Isaiah Saw
——— The ———
Glory of Jesus

LEWIS E. HILDRETH

ISAIAH SAW
THE
GLORY OF JESUS

© 2006 by Lewis E. Hildreth. All rights reserved.
2nd Printing 2014

Trusted Books is an imprint of Deep River Books. The views expressed or implied in this work are those of the author. To learn more about Deep River Books, go online to www.DeepRiverBooks.com.

No part of this publication may be reproduced, stored in a retrieval system or transmitted in any way by any means—electronic, mechanical, photocopy, recording or otherwise—without the prior permission of the copyright holder, except as provided by USA copyright law.

Unless otherwise noted, all Scriptures are taken from the Holy Bible, New International Version, Copyright © 1973, 1978, 1984 by the International Bible Society. Used by permission of Zondervan Publishing House. The "NIV" and "New International Version" trademarks are registered in the United States Patent and Trademark Office by International Bible Society.

Scripture references marked KJV are taken from the King James Version of the Bible.

ISBN: 978-1-63269-131-6
Library of Congress Catalog Card Number: 2006925188

"Isaiah said this because he saw Jesus' glory
and spoke about Him."
(John 12:41)

TABLE OF CONTENTS

Foreword		xi
Acknowledgements		xiii
Lesson 1:	Knowing God's Word	15
Lesson 2:	Preparing to Study Isaiah	
	How We View God and His Word	21
Lesson 3:	The Glory of the LORD	25
Lesson 4:	Here Am I; Send Me	33
Lesson 5:	Isaiah Chapter 1	
	Foreshadow of the Savior	39
	Knowledge and Understanding Critical	40
	The Holy One of God	41
	The Law is Important	42
	Our Daily Actions Count	44
Lesson 6:	Isaiah Chapters 2 Through 4	
	In the Last Days	47
	The Light Identified	48

	Trying to Escape	49
	The Branch	50
Lesson 7:	Isaiah Chapters 5 Through 7	
	What More Could He Do?	53
	Scoffing at God's Word	54
	Stand Firm in Your Faith	55
	The Virgin Birth	55
Lesson 8:	Isaiah Chapters 8 and 9	
	God Controls the Historical and Spiritual Outcomes	59
	Satan, Israel's Ultimate Enemy	61
	The Stone That Causes Men to Stumble	65
	The Prophetic Promise of the Savior	67
Lesson 9:	Isaiah Chapter 10	
	The Return to the Mighty God	69
Lesson 10:	Isaiah Chapters 11 Through 13	
	Jesus, the Branch	73
	The Coming Peace	75
	Salvation	76
	The Future Wrath of God	78
	Tribulation Survivors More Scarce Than Pure Gold	81
Lesson 11:	Isaiah Chapters 14 Through 16	
	Satan's Ambition	83
	Pride Goes Before a Fall	85
Lesson 12:	Isaiah Chapters 17 and 18	
	The Lord Comes for His Bride	89
	When the Trumpet Sounds	90
	The Jewish Holy Days:	
	Another Possibility for End Times Fulfillment	92
	The Bride of Christ	94
Lesson 13:	Isaiah Chapters 19 Through 24	
	Don't Be Caught Off Guard	97
	A Terrible Time on Earth	98
	What Happens to Christians?	99

Using Noah and Lot as Examples	100

Lesson 14: Isaiah Chapters 25 Through 28	
At the Renewal of All Things	103
We Are to Trust	104
The Triune God	105
Concerning the Resurrection	106
Israel to be Re-established in the Land	108

Lesson 15: Isaiah Chapters 29 Through 32	
Lip Service is Not Enough	111
Prophesy Only Good Things!	112
The Arm of the LORD	113
How Many Isaiahs?	115
Trusting Weapons or God	116
The Righteous Ruler	117

Lesson 16: Isaiah Chapters 34 Through 40	
All Nations Will Suffer	119
From Wrath to Joy	121
An Awesome Chapter; An Awesome God!	122
Trying to Understand Why	123
Creation or Evolution?	124
It is About the Savior	132

Lesson 17: Isaiah Chapters 41 and 42	
The Alpha and Omega	135
The Promise to Restore Israel	136
Jesus' True Identity Could Not be Mistaken	136
Just Look at the Evidence	138
Jesus is Introduced	139

Lesson 18: Isaiah Chapters 43 Through 45	
There is No Other God	141
Ancient Israel's Prophetic Future	142
God Promises to Regather	144
The Jews Are to Be God's Witnesses	145
The Fall of Babylon	146
God's Challenge to Us	148

Lesson 19: Isaiah Chapters 46 Through 51
    God's Faithfulness to Us   151
        The Ransom Price   153
        The Power of the Arm is Awesome   156

Lesson 20: Isaiah Chapters 52 and 53
    Mankind Will Be Without Excuse   159
        Beaten Beyond Recognition   161
        By His Wounds We Are Healed   162
        Jesus to the Rescue   167
        No Reason to Doubt the Promises   169

Lesson 21: Isaiah Chapters 54 Through 66
    Come to the Waters   171
        God's Word Will Accomplish His Desires   173
        The Kind of Fasting God Desires   174
        God Does Not Change   175
        The Lord's Timing   178
        The New Heaven and Earth   179

Names and Titles of Jesus   183

FOREWORD

One of the goals of this study is to highlight and reveal Jesus in Isaiah and throughout the Old Testament; to highlight the sameness (unity) of the message and completion of events—whether past, present or future—that knows no boundaries between the Old and New Testaments. Many Christians say "that's from the Old Testament," as if to say that it is basically irrelevant. This could not be further from the truth. The Old Testament is just as contemporary and relevant in thought, content and message as the New Testament. Remember, God is immutable (Malachi 3:6; Hebrews 13:8). His message does not change. The important doctrinal and spiritual ideals set forth in the New Testament were also recorded and taught in the Old Testament.

The Bible, both Old and New Testaments together, is the complete, inerrant, infallible Word of God, in its original language. Comparing Scriptures in Isaiah to other books of the Bible, both Old and New Testaments, is to show their consistency, constancy, completeness, and relevance to each other that is displayed over thousands of years by a myriad of writers, who were sometimes oblivious to the others' writings. This could not have happened naturally, by chance. It could only happen by Divine Revelation. All of the prophets testified that Divine

Revelation was how they received the information they wrote down. The Apostle Paul was no different. He testified in Galatians Chapter 1 that he received his instruction the same way. Galatians 1:11-12 says: *"I want you to know, brothers, that the gospel I preached is not something that man made up. I did not receive it from any man, nor was I taught it; rather, I received it by revelation from Jesus Christ."* We can trust the apostles' and prophets' message, their dedication to God, their honesty and their accuracy.

As you follow this study, it is strongly urged that you read along with all of the included Scripture references using your own Bible.

> *Scripture quotes used in this study are taken from The Holy Bible, New International Version (Copyright 1978 and 1984, New International Bible Society), unless otherwise noted. Capitalization of pronouns (i.e., "He," "His," "Him") has been added to clearly point out references to God and to Jesus.*

ACKNOWLEDGEMENTS

First, I give thanks to Almighty God and His Son Jesus for saving a sinner such as myself; having patience as I struggle from not knowing Him to having faith and confidence that He alone is my Source, for all that I am and know.

My heartfelt gratitude goes out to the following people for their assistance in this study project:

To my wife, Joy, who fills in the gaps in my writings. She was instrumental in getting this study out of my heart and mind and onto paper. It would not have happened without her. She is a work of God in my life.

To Marge Groover Wolfe, who was my ninth-grade English teacher before she was my great-aunt. Her aid with my grammar in this writing made up for what I should have learned in the ninth grade.

To Dr. David Barnhart, pastor, author, and founder of Abiding Word Ministries. His knowledge of Hebrew and of the subject of Jesus in the Old Testament gave me great encouragement that I was on the right track with this study.

To Mike Fraunfelter, a faithful Bible student and church youth leader, for his keen Scriptural insight and review of this manuscript.

Last, but certainly not least, to the many people whom I have been privileged to lead in Bible study groups over the years. The time spent in God's Word with these people has truly been a gift from God.

Lewis E. Hildreth

Lesson 1

KNOWING GOD'S WORD

In this study we will demonstrate with evidence from the Scriptures what kind of awesome God we worship. His abilities, power, knowledge, love, and other attributes go far beyond our ability to know and comprehend Him.

The New Testament writer Jude felt he had to write and urge us to *"contend for the faith that was once for all entrusted to the saints."* (Jude 3) This contending for, and defending of, the Word and faith is known as "apologetics." The word apologetics, in the original Greek form "apologia," means to *defend*, not apologize! If we are going to contend for the faith and defend it, we must be able to accurately discern and interpret God's written Word to us.

Many of you have, no doubt, encountered people who were very zealous in speaking to you about God. What they said might not have squared exactly with what you learned in Sunday School, but they surely were sincere and what they said made sense. It was logical and sounded reasonable. The Apostle Paul warns us about placing trust in what a person says just because of his sincerity and zeal for God. Speaking about his fellow Jews, Paul wrote in Romans 10:1-2: *"Brothers, my heart's desire and prayer to God for the Israelites is that they may be saved.*

*For I can testify about them that they are **zealous** for God, but their **zeal** is not based on **knowledge**."*

Now, the Jews had knowledge of God, just not *accurate* knowledge of God. The Apostle Paul knew of that about which he was talking. As he testifies in Philippians 3:4-6, trained as a Pharisee, he had both zeal and knowledge of God. This Pharisaical training started when he was a young child, and continued into adulthood. This training was similar in many ways to training for the priesthood, with in-depth study in Scripture, as well as Mosaic and rabbinic laws. He found out during his Damascus Road experience, however, that his knowledge of God was inaccurate and his zeal misplaced. That is how he could say what he did about his fellow Jews concerning their knowledge of God, and their zeal.

Therefore, zeal and sincerity is not the litmus test for accurate knowledge of God. We always have to take what a person says about God back to the Word of God for our confirmation…because people can be sincerely wrong.

Their zeal may not be based on accurate knowledge of God. There is nothing wrong with being zealous for God. Zeal and passion are admirable traits for the Christian; just make sure it is for the right reasons.

As much as possible, let Scripture interpret and explain Scripture. Most people have an opinion about what the Bible says. The Bible teacher must be able to back up his or her statements with Scripture and know where to find them. If you cannot back it up with Scripture, and be able to find it, then don't say it! Otherwise your credibility could be in trouble and credibility is everything in teaching the Bible.

This study will follow the "high view" of Scripture, as opposed to the "low view." The high view holds that the Bible is the inerrant and infallible Word of God in its original languages (Hebrew, Aramaic and Greek). It is "*God-breathed and is useful for teaching, rebuking, correcting and training in righteousness, so that the man of God may be thoroughly equipped for every good work."* (II Timothy 3:16) If we let the Bible flow in a natural, literal way as we read and study it, then our natural conclusion will be the high view. Thus, we will use the literal method of interpretation, recognizing that types, metaphors, symbols and allegories are found throughout the Bible. These are used to explain and expound upon the literal message of Scripture.

Many scholars hold to the allegorical method of interpretation. However, if it is not used in context with the literal meaning, this method can be abused. The allegorical method is often used to change the literal meaning into anything the user wants it to be, effectively rewriting the Bible. Early church theologians used this method as an attempt to replace Israel with the Church. They took the Old Testament promises made to the Jewish people, to Israel, and allegorically changed the promises made to Israel, claiming them for the Church. Today, this practice continues and is called "replacement theology." This theology teaches that the rebirth of the state of Israel has nothing to do with the fulfillment of prophecy; that the Jewish people are no longer God's chosen people; that the Church is the true Israel. As a result of this, some even claim that Israel does not have a right to exist. Because of the misuse of the allegorical method, many Christians are led astray where prophecy is concerned. We must take the Bible seriously as well as literally. Those who allegorize everything do not seem to take the Bible seriously as a document from God.

The literal method demands that words say what they mean and mean what they say. All secondary meanings of Scripture—whether allegories, types, parables or symbols—depend on their initial, literal meaning and context for their definition and existence. The literal method is the only way we can keep a check on the imaginations of people, and their intentional (or unintentional) perversions of Holy Scripture and its true meaning. It is said that no prophecy that has been completely fulfilled, has been fulfilled in any other way but literally.

Now, when we speak of the literal method of interpretation, this method is not captive to a single fulfillment. Most prophecies have a "dual aspect." This "dual aspect," however, does not mean "dual meaning." "Dual aspect" is a reference to fulfillment of the prophecy. When the prophets spoke and recorded God's words to them, it was usually a message to the people of that prophet's time, though sometimes it was a message of hope that applied to some point in the future, even the distant future. The message generally had relevance to their immediate moral and spiritual condition, and it warned of the consequences of their depraved moral and spiritual condition, in the form of God's judgment and punishment.

The reason for God's judgment and punishment was, as God told Ezekiel, *"That they will know that I am the LORD."* The Israelites had strayed so far from the decrees they had received from God through Moses, that they no longer knew who God was and thus lost their fear of, and respect for, Him. So the message was for the prophet's own time. Next, with God being outside the frame of time, He was able to look down the timeline to a period of time in the distant future to the prophet and see circumstances and conditions very similar, or identical, to the conditions that the prophet saw and was experiencing. Therefore, God was able to foresee that the single literal meaning could and would have a dual fulfillment. So the message given to the prophets from God would always be a message to the prophet's own generation and could also be a message to a generation in the distant future. The prophets understood the difference between one-time prophecies and dual fulfillment concerning Christ.

Peter understood this when he wrote in I Peter 1:10-12, *"Concerning this salvation, the prophets, who spoke of the grace that was to come to you, searched intently and with the greatest care, trying to find out the time and circumstances to which the spirit of Christ in them was pointing, when He predicted the suffering of Christ and the glories that would follow. It was revealed to them that they were not serving themselves but you, when they spoke of the things that have now been told you by those who have preached the gospel to you by the Holy Spirit sent from heaven. Even angels long to look into these things."* They knew the event was going to happen, they just didn't know when, and neither do we.

Since we're talking about the prophets, how can you tell a true prophet of God from a false one? How would you make the determination? If they are 60 percent right in what they say? Or maybe 90 percent? God gives us the answers to these questions. Deuteronomy 13:1-4 tells us: *"If a prophet, or one who foretells by dreams appears among you and announces to you a miraculous sign or wonder, and if the sign or wonder of which he has spoken takes place, and he says, let us follow other gods (gods you have not known) and let us worship them, you must not listen to the words of that prophet or dreamer. The LORD your God is testing you to find out whether you love Him with all your heart and with all your soul. It is the LORD your God you must follow, and Him you must revere. Keep His commands and obey Him; serve Him and hold fast to Him."* Then, in Deuteronomy 18:20-22, we read: *"But a prophet who presumes to speak in My Name anything I have not commanded him to say, or a prophet who speaks in the name of other gods, must be put to death. You may say to yourselves, 'How can we know when a message has not been spoken by the* LORD?' *If what a prophet proclaims in the Name of the* LORD *does not take place or come true, that is a message the* LORD *has not spoken. That prophet has spoken presumptuously. Do not be afraid of him."*

We have allowed God's Word to answer the question. First, the prophet has to be 100 percent right. Not 60 percent, not 90 percent, but 100 percent. If it is not 100 percent right, it has not come from the LORD. And if it is 100 percent correct, but the prophet tries to lead you away from the one true God, the God of the Bible, then he also is a false prophet. These guidelines, given in the days of Moses, apply to our day as well.

When God speaks to His prophets, is that a promise, or a prediction, or just some cosmic fortune-telling? We can rule out fortune-telling because God warns us in Leviticus not to consult with mediums and spiritualists. It is not from God. If one would make a prediction about the outcome of a football game, you could be right or you could be wrong, but at best it is just an educated guess. But when God speaks to His prophets, it is reliable and trustworthy; it is a promise. God made a promise to Abraham, which also included a prophecy that He would make of him a great nation. It is a prophetic promise. Complete fulfillment is just a matter of time. He made similar prophetic promises to Noah, to Jacob/Israel, Joseph and others.

<u>God cannot go back on His promises</u>. If He did, He would be a liar. About the unbelieving Jewish people, Romans 11:28-29 says: *"As far as the gospel is concerned, they are enemies on your account; but as far as election is concerned, they are loved on account of the patriarchs, for* **God's gifts and His call are irrevocable**." Those who hold to "replacement theology" are at risk of making God out as a liar, because He plainly says His gifts and His call are irrevocable. This is a promise.

As this study focuses on the book of Isaiah, we will be constantly comparing the Scriptures in Isaiah with other books of the Bible, both Old and New Testaments, as well as other historical writings. These comparisons will show how prophecies made by Isaiah were fulfilled in the New Testament. Sometimes the comparisons will show similarities of circumstances that the writers encountered. Sometimes they are direct quotes, and in some cases quoted by Jesus Himself. When Jesus quotes from the Old Testament, He verifies the prophets' writings as accurate. Also, sometimes, when Jesus and/or some of the New Testament writers quote and explain from the Old Testament, it is to reveal something that had previously been hidden.

When all of this is put together, the comparing of Scripture—Old Testament to New Testament—will show the amazing continuity of meaning and content that the Bible has. It will show the overwhelming consistency among all Bible writers, saying the same things in different words, across the centuries, in an undeniable unity of thought, unity of prophecy, and unity of message, giving us hope and faith for all times and all circumstances. This is not duplicated in any other so-called "holy book!" The Bible is the complete Word of God, given to man, from Genesis to Revelation.

Faith Questions

1. Why is it important to allow Scripture to explain and interpret Scripture?
2. What did the Apostle Paul say about his fellow Jews' zeal for God?
3. What are the hallmarks of God's true prophets?
4. How can you tell if a prophet is a false one?

Lesson 2

PREPARING TO STUDY ISAIAH
HOW WE VIEW GOD AND HIS WORD

In this study of Isaiah, the many different ways Isaiah saw the pre-existent, pre-incarnate Son of God, Jesus, will be shown. Isaiah and King David had the pre-incarnate Jesus revealed to them like no other prophets. There are many "code" words that point to Jesus and once we learn Isaiah's use of them, then Isaiah will come alive to the reader as never before.

Before we actually get into the study of Isaiah, a few things need to be clarified. Some scholars attribute the authorship of the book of Isaiah to "three Isaiahs." They have divided the book into three sections, and claim because of the style and the time frame about which each section is written, that one man could not have authored it by himself. They claim someone who was living at the time these events were written about simply recorded history and inserted it into the book called Isaiah. If this is true, then how could any Isaiah give such a detailed account of Jesus' crucifixion in Chapter 53, and elsewhere in his book, 750 years before it took place? There simply was no eyewitness account of the crucifixion inserted into Isaiah, as is verified by the Dead Sea Scrolls.

This begs the question: How big is the God of these scholars? How big is your God? Is your God capable of communicating with men? Some scholars seem to think not. Can your God stand outside of the timeline and then look at time from the beginning to the end? Is He capable of knowing what is going to happen along the timeline, at any point in time, with any historical event—past, present, future? Is He all-knowing enough to know every person ever born or who will be born, and what each will do with his life? Is He capable of creating the cosmos?

If God isn't capable of these things, then the Bible is just a collection of old writings with no relevance to good or bad, right or wrong. If He is not capable of resurrecting people from the dead, then as the Apostle Paul explains in I Corinthians 15:13: *"If there is no resurrection of the dead, then not even Christ has been raised. And if Christ has not been raised, our preaching is useless and so is your faith."* Again, Paul says in 15:17: *"And if Christ has not been raised, your faith is futile; you are still in your sins. Then those who have fallen asleep in Christ are lost. If only for this life we have hope in Christ, we are to be pitied more than all men."*

If there is no God, then there is no right or wrong. If there is no God, then right and wrong become relative. Every person, society, and nation is free to make up its own laws and ideas of what is right and wrong. In current historical times, "ethnic cleansing" (a very clinical and sanitary term for killing and persecuting ethnic groups) becomes what is accepted for society to do. If there is no God, then it is okay to rewrite history, rewrite the Bible to make it say what is morally acceptable to the culture at the time, or to just deny that God even exists, and relegate the Bible to a collection of ancient writings that have no bearing on modern thought and cultures. Following are some examples in specific fields of study.

If there is no God in biology, than all things evolved by blind chance. Using God as an explanation of origins is not acceptable. An unborn child becomes known as a "fetus" or "blob of tissue." (Did you know that "fetus" comes from a Latin word meaning "little one?") It is "acceptable" to use stem cells from aborted babies for research, even though there has never been any medical cures discovered using these stem cells.

If there is no God in education, then we can do away with school prayer; even make it unconstitutional. We can expel children that bow their head in prayer and punish them for reading the Bible at lunchtime. We can teach them how to be sexually promiscuous, how to get and use contraceptives, and where to go for an abortion; all without parental knowledge and consent. The homosexual lifestyle is taught as being normal and accepted and even promoted as a good thing.

If there is no God in the social sciences, then the social sciences can support abortion, easy divorce and living together. In the social sciences, there are no wrong answers, no moral absolutes.

If there is no God in the field of law, then our judicial system can legalize the killing of unborn babies and euthanasia, prevent student prayer, or prohibit the display of the Ten Commandments in public schools and other public places. It can also prevent credible evidence for Intelligent Design from being taught in public schools.

Abraham Lincoln once said: "No law gives me the right to do what is wrong." If there is no God in the field of history, then we can rewrite the textbooks to remove God and remove all reference to the Christian ethic that so strongly motivated the founders of our country.

If there is no God in the field of art and Hollywood entertainment, then anything goes. Graphic displays of pornography and adultery, on the Internet, TV and in the movies, along with public displays reducing Jesus Himself and the symbols of Christianity to the gutter, are all considered "art." Video games and rap music glorify the killing of cops, the raping of women, and other practiced forms of human depravity.

It doesn't matter how any of this psychologically harms children or offends Christians, it must be protected and defended at all costs.

If there is no God in the field of environmentalism, then plants and animals become more important than human beings. You can get a heavy fine and even jail time for destroying eagle eggs, but destroying a pre-born human from its embryonic stage, all the way up to partial-birth abortion, is environmentally favorable and expedient.

If there is no God in the field of journalism, then journalism will support, validate and give credence to all of the "moral and ethical values" of the fields above. After all, they are in league with each other and will support each other's agendas.

Oh, the power of the press, television, and movies! The media, in all its forms, has the ability to substitute lies for the truth and can relegate the so-called "archaic" ethical and moral worldview of the God of the Bible, and of Bible-believing Christians, to the trash heap of history. Christians can then be portrayed and labeled as intolerant, hateful, bigoted, ignorant, uneducated, unreasonable, laughable, and without merit or value. Labeling people you hate, or disagree with, allows you to marginalize or dismiss what they say without ever having to confront the truthfulness of their position. This technique is used in the liberal media to great effect.

It is amazing to see how the liberal church so often comes down on the side of the liberal, godless worldview. Many who call themselves Christians have a view of the world that doesn't stray far from the world's view of things. The polls say 80 percent of Americans identify themselves as Christian. Thirty-eight percent of these responded that they had been to church in the past seven days. Isaiah records in Chapter 29:13: *"The Lord says: 'These people come near to Me with their mouth and honor Me with their lips. But their hearts are far from Me. Their worship of Me is made up only of rules taught by men.'"* Are we, in this country, like the people Isaiah is speaking about?

The fields listed above are not all-inclusive, but these examples are intended to help us see the godless foundation and core beliefs that in most cases are representative of the moral and ethical worldview that is dominant within our culture.

Christians have often been asked, "What right do you have to force of your moral and religious views down our throats?" With that question, and with a sense of fairness, many Christians withdraw from the fray on morality. But morality abhors a vacuum. When Christians remove their morality from the marketplace of ideas, the world will rush to fill the vacuum with their own moral values. You will not like what you will get. Indeed, consider what we have had crammed down *our* throats already! In this country, you have every right to stand up for what you believe, and should do so passionately; otherwise the world will soon take that right away. They will make it illegal to publicly speak out on certain moral issues. This has already happened in Canada.

Faith Questions

1. Who determines what is right or wrong? Explain your answer.
2. Do you think you should have a part in the debate about what is right or wrong?

Lesson 3

The Glory of the LORD

*"Isaiah said this because he saw Jesus' glory **and spoke about Him**."* (John 12:41) How did Isaiah see Jesus' glory? Some of the prophets, like Daniel and Ezekiel, had God revealed to them through dreams and visions. Moses had a physical encounter with the living God (Exodus 3:2-6). Isaiah testifies in Chapter 6 that he "...*saw the Lord seated on a throne, high and exalted, and the train of His robe filled the temple.*" In other places Isaiah "hears the LORD," or as he sometimes says, "*the Word of the* LORD *came to me.*" At other times, the "hearing" and the "seeing" occurred together. Whatever Isaiah saw, and heard, it must have been fantastic.

The Apostle Paul had a **vision** of heaven, recorded in II Corinthians Chapter 12, in which he "...***heard*** *inexpressible things, things that a man is not permitted to tell."* In Ezekiel Chapter 1, the Prophet Ezekiel describes the **vision** he had by the Kebar River in the land of the Babylonians. Beginning in verse 26, Ezekiel tries to describe what he saw. He says: *"Above the expanse over their heads was what looked like a throne of sapphire, and high above the throne was a figure **like that of a man**. I **saw** that from what appeared to be His waist up He looked like glowing metal, as if full of fire, and that from there down He looked like fire; and a brilliant*

25

*light surrounded Him. Like the appearance of a rainbow in the clouds on a rainy day, so was the radiance around Him. This was the appearance of the likeness of the **Glory of the LORD.**"*

In Revelation Chapter 1 the Apostle John gives a very similar description of a heavenly Being. Verses 12-18 read: *"I turned around to see the voice that was speaking to me. And when I turned I saw seven golden lampstands, and among the lampstands was someone "**like a Son of Man**," dressed in a robe reaching down to His feet and with a golden sash around His chest. His head and hair were white like wool, as white as snow, and His eyes were like blazing fire. His feet were like bronze glowing in a furnace, and His voice was like the sound of rushing waters. In His right hand He held seven stars, and out of His mouth came a sharp double-edged sword. His face was like the sun shining in all its brilliance. When I saw Him, I fell at His feet as though dead. Then He placed His right hand on me and said: 'Do not be afraid. I am the First and the Last. I am the Living One; I was dead, and behold I am alive for ever and ever! And I hold the keys of death and Hades.'"*

When Ezekiel saw this likeness of the **Glory of the LORD**, he fell face down, just like John, and he **heard** the voice of One speaking.

This **"likeness of the Glory of the LORD"** first appears in Exodus 16:10. *"While Aaron was speaking to the whole Israelite community, they looked toward the desert, and there was the **Glory of the LORD** in the cloud."* The **Glory of the LORD** in Exodus 16:10, the **Angel of God** in Exodus 14:19 and the **Angel of the LORD** in Genesis 22:15 are all three recorded in many other places in the Old Testament, and are used interchangeably. All possess the same deistic – or "God-like" qualities, and most times speak as though they were God. (Judges 2:1-5, 13:2-22) Ordinary angels are created beings, and although they possess great and supernatural powers, they do not possess God-like qualities. Only God has God-like qualities. These three speak for God in the first person, and only God speaks for God in the first person. The **Glory of the Lord**, **Angel of God**, and **Angel of the LORD** are descriptive titles used by the ancient Old Testament writers to describe the **visible** presence and interactions of God with men. The question then becomes: which of the three manifestations of God – Father, Son, or Holy Spirit, do these three titles pertain to?

The Glory of the LORD

We know the pre-incarnate Jesus—*Yeshua* (His Hebrew name)—was present during the Israelites' exodus from Egypt, as the Apostle Paul records in I Corinthians 10:1-4: *"For I do not want you to be ignorant of the fact, brothers, that our forefathers were all under the cloud and that they all passed through the sea. They were all baptized into Moses in the cloud and in the sea. They all ate the same spiritual food and drank the same spiritual drink; for they drank from the spiritual Rock that accompanied them, and that Rock was* **Christ***."* Jude verse 5 also gives a testimony to the pre-incarnate presence of Jesus: *"Though you already know all this, I want to remind you that the Lord delivered His people out of Egypt, but later destroyed those who did not believe."* Some early manuscripts use "Jesus" instead of "Lord." "Lord" is synonymous to Jesus in the Epistle writings of the New Testament.

The **"Angel of the LORD" and the "Glory of the LORD" are both referring to none other than Jesus Christ, the Son of God, in His pre-incarnate** (Old Testament) **form.**

Hebrews 1:3 states: *"The Son is the* **radiance** *of God's* **glory***...."* This radiance is the visible, recognizable representation of the exact likeness and essence of God's glory. This exact likeness and essence of God is more than just a photo copy. Jesus literally, and in entirety, possesses the same attributes and glory that His Father possesses. **Jesus was, and is, the Glory of His Father, the Glory of Yahweh, the Glory of the LORD.** Whenever you read the **"Glory of the LORD"** in the Old Testament, read it as the pre-incarnate essence and presence of Jesus.

Another time when we can see this "likeness of the **Glory of the LORD**" is in II Chronicles 7:1. Here, Solomon had just completed building the temple and just finished his prayer of dedication. *"When Solomon finished praying, fire came down from heaven and consumed the burnt offering and the sacrifices, and the* **Glory of the LORD** *filled the temple. The priest could not enter the temple of the LORD because the* **Glory of the LORD** *filled it. When all the Israelites saw the fire coming down and the* **Glory of the LORD** *above the temple, they knelt on the pavement with their faces to the ground and they worshiped and gave thanks to the* LORD*, saying, 'He is good; His love endures forever.'"*

This **Glory of the LORD**, this presence of God, the pre-incarnate Jesus, remained in the temple through thick and thin, through good times and bad times, even though the actions and sinful behavior of the Israelite people, their worshipping of false gods and idols, and sacrificing of their children on the altar of Molech (Jeremiah 32:25), hurt and angered God greatly. God had sent prophets to the Israelite people during the more than 400 years between Solomon and the destruction of the city of Jerusalem and the temple by the Babylonians in 587 B.C. God pleaded with them to turn away from their destructive lifestyle and to return to Him, the one true God, to follow His laws and decrees, all to no avail.

Just before the destruction of the temple, God took Ezekiel in visions to Jerusalem, to the temple. In Ezekiel 9:3, the prophet describes what he saw. *"Now the* **Glory of the God of Israel** *went up from above the cherubim, where it had been, and moved to the threshold of the temple."* God was starting to pull His presence from the temple and the city. Ezekiel 10:18 further describes this departure. *"Then the* **Glory of the LORD** *departed from over the threshold of the temple and stopped above the cherubim. While I watched, the cherubim spread their wings and rose from the ground, and as they went, the wheels went with them. They stopped at the entrance to the east gate of the* LORD*'s house, and the* **Glory of the God of Israel** *was above them."*

Next, in Ezekiel 11:23, the **Glory of the LORD** went up from within the city and stopped above the mountain east of it. This mountain east of the city of Jerusalem is the Mount of Olives. So the glory and presence of God went from the Holy of Holies in the temple, to the threshold or doorway of the temple, to the East Gate of the city wall which leads to the temple, and then to the mountain east of Jerusalem. When this **Glory of the LORD**, this presence of God, this essence of Jesus, left the temple and the city, God took His hedge of protection for the city with Him. Very shortly after this event, the Babylonians came and destroyed the city and its empty shell of a building that once housed the indwelling glory and essence of God, known as the temple.

We are also just "empty shells" if we do not have the Glory and essence of God dwelling in us. Without the indwelling Glory, we also will be subject to destruction, just as the temple was. According to Ezekiel, this **Glory of the LORD** would not enter the temple again until after the establishment of the State of Israel (which occurred in 1948), after the Tribulation period, and coinciding with the Second Coming of Jesus Christ.

The Glory of the Lord

Ezekiel 43:1 says: *"Then the man brought me to the gate facing east, and I saw the **Glory of the God of Israel** coming from the east."* Verse 4 states: *"The **Glory of the LORD** entered the temple through the gate facing east."* In Zechariah 14:2-4, the Prophet Zechariah confirms Ezekiel's statements and adds a few more details: *"I will gather all the nations to Jerusalem to fight against it... Then the LORD will go out and fight against those nations, as He fights in the day of battle. On that day His feet will **stand on the Mount of Olives**, east of Jerusalem, and the Mount of Olives will be split in two from east to west...."*

The Gospels record that Jesus left the Mount of Olives, east of Jerusalem, on the day we know as "Palm Sunday." Jesus, along with His procession, crossed the Kidron Valley and entered through the East Gate into the temple. He entered as the sacrificial Lamb, but was this the time in history that these two prophecies from Ezekiel and Zechariah were looking forward to? To answer this question, let's turn to Acts 1:9-12. *"After He (Jesus) said this, He was taken up before their very eyes, and the cloud hid Him from their sight. They were looking intently up into the sky as He was going, when suddenly two men dressed in white stood beside them. 'Men of Galilee,' they said, 'why do you stand here looking into the sky? This same Jesus, who has been taken from you into heaven, will come back in the same way you have seen Him go into heaven.' **Then they returned to Jerusalem from the hill called the Mount of Olives**...."* The Glory of the LORD, Jesus, will return to the Mount of Olives and once again enter through the gate facing east, into the temple, as He destroys all those nations who come against Jerusalem.

If one were to go to Jerusalem today, and visit what is left of the old city wall, or perhaps see pictures of it, you will find the East Gate. There is some-thing unusual about this gate, in that it is sealed with very large and heavy stones. It is sealed up tight! It was sealed by the Muslims shortly after their invasion of the land around 800 A D. Directly in front of the East Gate is a Muslim cemetery. In 1917 during World War I, General Allenby of Britain had the city surrounded by his forces. He was expecting stiff resistance from the Turkish (Muslim) occupiers. Before the invasion was to begin, General Allenby had planes fly over Jerusalem, dropping leaflets. The leaflets said (paraphrased), "You are surrounded. Surrender your arms and you will be treated well," and they were signed "General Allenby." The Turkish forces, in order to better defend their positions, were about to knock down the stones that sealed the East Gate. When the leaflets were dropped, most could not read the English very well and thought the leaflets were signed by "Allah." This incident, along with other operations around Jerusalem directed by General Allenby, isolated Jerusalem, and the Turkish forces surrendered the city without firing a shot. The gate remained sealed.

In 1967, the East Gate was in the Arab sector of the divided city of Jerusalem. The Arabs had set a date to unseal the East Gate. The day before they planned to unseal the East Gate, the 1967 Arab-Israeli war (known as the Six-Day War) broke out. The East Gate remained sealed, and it is sealed to this day.

In Chapter 44:1-3, Ezekiel has this to say: *"Then the man brought me back to the **outer gate of the sanctuary, the one facing east**, and it was **shut**. The LORD said to me, 'This gate is to remain **shut**. It must not be opened; no one may enter through it. It is to remain **shut** because the LORD, the God of Israel, has entered through it. The Prince Himself is the only one who may sit inside the gateway to eat in the presence of the LORD. He is to enter by way of the portico of the gateway and go out the same way.'"*

This gate will remain sealed until the Second Coming of Jesus Christ. Psalm 118:20 says: *"This is the gate of the LORD through which the righteous may enter."* When Jesus Christ comes back and sets His feet on the Mount of Olives, there will again be another Palm Sunday procession. Continuing in Psalm 118:22-27: *"The stone the builders rejected has become the Capstone; the LORD has done this, and it is marvelous in our eyes. This is the day the LORD has made; let us rejoice and be glad in it. O LORD, save us; O LORD, grant us success."* On the original Palm Sunday, the people said, and people will say at His Second Coming: *"Blessed is He who comes in the Name of the LORD. From the house of the LORD we bless you. The LORD is God, and He has made His light shine upon us.* ***With boughs in hand, join in the festal procession up to the horns of the altar.*** *You are my God, and I will give You thanks; You are my God, and I will exalt You."*

The vision of a figure of a man that represented the likeness of the Glory of the LORD that Ezekiel had, and the description he gave, is the same vision that the Apostle John saw and wrote about in Revelation

Chapter 1. John identified this figure of a man as the resurrected Lord Jesus. The Apostle John had the same reaction that Ezekiel had: he fell face down at His feet as though dead. They were both in awe of what they saw, overwhelmed and fearful, not knowing what to expect, not knowing what was coming next. What they were seeing was literally out of this world. This was a close encounter with the living God, and their lives would never be the same again.

The Apostle Paul also had an encounter with the living God on the road to Damascus. The epistles Paul wrote testify to the total change of his attitude, goals, direction, and even beliefs about God, which such an experience brings about. We also can encounter the living and resurrected Son of God, Jesus, and turn our lives around through studying His Word, dedicating our lives to His service, turning away from sin and following Him. This is the profound effect He has on people who truly seek Him. This was the profound effect he had on Ezekiel, Isaiah, Paul and John.

What these men saw and experienced was something that had the same effect on Abraham, Moses, and all the great men and women of the Bible. They dedicated the remainder of their lives to absolute commitment, obedience, and service to God. What these men saw, Isaiah included, caused their ancient language to fail them. Our language would fail us as well, trying to describe an indescribable scene. They were at a loss for words, just as we would be, at such an awesome, overwhelming sight.

Isaiah records in 6:1: *"In the year that King Uzziah died, I saw the Lord seated on a throne high and exalted, and the train of His robe filled the temple."* Remember how the Glory of the LORD filled Solomon's temple at its dedication? Here, just the train of His robe is enough to fill the temple. Then Isaiah goes on to describe what he saw, but he does not attempt to give as many details as John and Ezekiel. Perhaps he thought it would be an exercise in futility! The Apostle John records in John 12:41 that Isaiah *"saw Jesus' glory and spoke about Him."*

All of this is to demonstrate that the pre-incarnate Jesus was active in His involvement and interaction in the lives of His called and chosen people, and in revealing Himself to His prophets in a very personal way.

For believers today, Jesus is still very involved in our lives, and continues to reveal Himself to us as we seek to know Him better.

Faith Questions

1. How was the vision experienced by Ezekiel similar to John's vision in Revelation?
2. What was the result of the Glory of the LORD leaving the temple, and Jerusalem?
3. What will be the result when the Glory of the LORD returns to Jerusalem from the Mount of Olives?

Lesson 4

HERE AM I; SEND ME

In the previous lesson, Isaiah 6:1 was quoted. This is where it is recorded that Isaiah saw the Lord, seated on a throne high and exalted, and the train of His robe filled the temple. It was discussed earlier that this vision Isaiah saw was of the pre-incarnate Lord Jesus, and there was some evidence given as to how this could be. Another evidence lies in the translation.

In Matthew Chapter 22, the Pharisees and Sadducees tried to trap Jesus with their questioning. They were not successful. Then Jesus decided to turn the tables on them and ask them some questions concerning the Christ. In verse 41, while the Pharisees were gathered together, Jesus asked them, *"'What do you think about the Christ? Whose Son is He?' 'The Son of David,' they replied. He said to them, 'How is it then that David, speaking by the Spirit, calls Him Lord? For he says, 'The Lord said to my Lord, sit at My right hand until I put Your enemies under Your feet.' If then David calls Him Lord, how could He be his son?' No one could say a word in reply, and from that day on no one dared to ask Him any more questions."*

In the above verse, Jesus is quoting Psalm 110. In the Jewish culture at the time of Jesus and earlier, a man would never call his own first-born son, or any son for that matter, "Lord." If the Christ were truly David's son, David would not refer to Him as "my Lord." In the Jewish culture the first-born son was equal to his father. He could sign contracts, buy land, conduct any kind of business, with the full weight and authority of his father behind him. It was the same as his father doing it himself. This is why, when Jesus said He was the Son of God, the high priest and other Jewish authorities wanted to kill Him. By claiming to be the Son of God, He was claiming to be equal to God, which was blasphemous in their eyes and deserving of death. When Jesus asked the Sadducees and the Pharisees these questions concerning David calling the Christ "Lord," they knew their weak and inaccurate theology could not overcome the rightly-divined Word of God given by Jesus. So they gave no answer. However, this question goes to the heart of who the Christ is. When Jesus is quoting Psalm 110, there is a conversation going on between two Lords. Let's turn to Psalm 110 and examined this issue more closely.

Verse 1 of Psalm 110 starts by saying: *"The **LORD** said to my **Lord**."* Notice the first **"LORD"** is all capital letters, and the second **"Lord"** only has the "L" capitalized. How can this be explained? If you would look at the preface of your Bible, you will find an explanation given of the translation from Hebrew to English. The divine name ***YHVH*** (the unpronounceable Hebrew Name of God), commonly referred to as the Tetragrammaton (which means "four characters"), is always translated as **LORD**, with all capital letters. This direct translation is used by most English versions.

The other Hebrew word translated as **Lord** is ***Adonai***. This "Lord" only has one capital letter. You'll need to learn to watch for this important distinction when reading King David's Psalms, and the book of Isaiah. Looking at the quote in Psalm 110:1, and substituting the Hebrew words for "LORD" and "Lord," we find that **YHVH** (YAHWEH) says to **Adonai**: *"Sit at My right hand until I make Your enemies a footstool for Your feet."* **YHVH** is always the Hebrew for God the Father. God is not talking to Himself. He is having a conversation with the pre-incarnate Jesus.

This can be demonstrated in Hebrews 1:13: *"For to which of the angels did God ever say, 'Sit at My right hand until I make Your enemies a footstool for Your feet.'"*? God did not say this to an angel; He said this to His Son – **Adonai**, Jesus. All of Hebrews Chapter 1 is focusing on why Jesus is not an angel. This whole chapter is about Jesus, about Him being God the Son, and it is clear that God the Father was addressing His Son in verse 13, which quotes Psalm 110:1. This chapter in Hebrews should also clear up that Jesus is not, and never was, an angel. The Old Testament description of the "**Angel of the LORD,**" which had deistic qualities, was an attempt by the ancient writers to describe what they did not fully understand about this Spirit being. It was not an angel, but the pre-incarnate Christ they were seeing.

In our study of Isaiah it will become clear that Isaiah, as well as King David, made the distinction between these two Names of God, and used them appropriately. This cannot be said of the other prophets, who use these two names interchangeably; therefore, distinctions between the Father and the Son cannot be made in the writings of the other prophets. These distinctions between the two Names of God only work with King David's Psalms and the book of Isaiah. As mentioned before, Isaiah and King David had the pre-incarnate Jesus revealed to them like no other prophets.

Most scholars will object to using **Adonai** for anything other than a name for God, one among several names used to identify God in the Old Testament. This is true in most cases. But Isaiah is different. **Adonai** (**Lord**) will be translated as Jesus. **YHVH** (**LORD**) will be translated as God the Father, or the Father. Keep this in mind as you follow along in your Bible. You be the judge as to whether this is an acceptable interpretation for God's Word as recorded in Isaiah. We will discuss in more detail the different names and titles for God and Jesus found in Isaiah as we progress further into the study.

A couple of references have been made to Isaiah Chapter 6 already, so let's return one more time and revisit what Isaiah saw. He said, *"I saw the **Lord** seated high and exalted, and the train of His robe filled the temple."* If you will notice what is capitalized in the name "**Lord**," and refer to the just-mentioned translation points, what you will see is that Isaiah, as recorded in John 12:41, saw **Adonai**, Jesus the Lord, in all His glory; seated high and exalted, and the train of His robe filled the temple.

Isaiah continues describing his vision with fear and trepidation. He continues in verse 5, "*'Woe is me!' I cried. 'I am ruined! For I am a man of unclean lips, and I live among a people of unclean lips, and my eyes have seen the King, the* **Lord** *Almighty.' Then one of the seraphs flew to me with a live coal in his hand, which he had taken with tongs from the altar. With that he touched my mouth and said, 'See, this has touched your lips; your guilt is taken away and your sin atoned for.'"* Here we see the future atoning work of Jesus, as Isaiah is being prepared for the mission God is calling him to do. Verse 8 says *"Then I heard the voice of the* **Lord** *saying, 'Who shall I send? Who will go for Us?'"* **Adonai**—Jesus—didn't say "Who will go for Me," but "Who will go for US?" (plural). And Isaiah said, "'*Here am I. Send me!' And He said, 'Go and tell this people…*'"

Isaiah heard the voice of Who? **Adonai**, Jesus, the Lord! When Isaiah volunteered, as we must volunteer, the command to **GO** and tell is very similar to the command found in Matthew 28:19: *"Therefore* **GO** *and make disciples of all nations.…"* Isaiah had been born spiritually dead, but now he was spiritually alive. This is similar to, if not the same as, the born-again experience that we have. We are born "dead" as well, but the born-again experience makes us spiritually alive. We are truly "born again" from above.

Isaiah said "yes" to Jesus and crossed over from death to life (John 5:24). When we say "yes" to Jesus, we pass from death to eternal life. Isaiah said *"Here am I, send me."* Romans 10:13-15 says: *"Everyone who calls on the Name of the Lord will be saved. How, then, can they call on the One they have not believed in? And how can they believe in the One of whom they have not heard? And how can they hear without someone preaching to them? And how can they preach* **unless they are sent?***…"*

Will you say to the Lord, "Here am I, send me?" Send me to the people who are ever hearing, but never understanding; ever seeing, but never perceiving. Send me to the factory, to the school, to the university, to my family, to the grain elevator, to the military, to the mission field; to the little country church where people have been warming the pews for forty or more years but never hearing the message of salvation. Jesus is still asking, "Who will go for Us? Will it be you?"

Isaiah had his vision. He was made aware of his sinful, unclean condition. He had his sins atoned for, and was called to the mission field of his home country (for which he enthusiastically volunteered), all here in Isaiah Chapter 6. It seems as though Chapter 6 ought to be placed at the very beginning of the book. It might seem somewhat out of place, since Isaiah (or anyone) must be called by God and equipped to discharge the gift or gifts God has given them before they start their ministry. In Isaiah's case it was the gift of prophecy. However, this study will start with the traditional first chapter of Isaiah.

When Isaiah so enthusiastically said "Here am I, send me," he had fire in his belly. He had fire in his heart. Jeremiah spoke of a similar condition in his book, in 20:8-9: *"Whenever I speak, I cry out proclaiming violence and destruction. So the Word of the* LORD *has brought me insult and reproach all day long. But if I say, I will not mention Him or speak anymore in His Name,* **His Word is in my heart like a burning fire shut up in my bones. I am weary of holding it in; indeed, I cannot."** This is the experience we should have when we invite the Lord Jesus Christ into our hearts. We should have a fire in our heart that cannot be extinguished.

Have you invited the Lord into your heart? Have you received the "tongues of fire," the Holy Spirit, into your heart? If you haven't, God is waiting. Why not do it now?

Faith Questions

1. Why did Jesus quote Psalm 110:1 when confronting the Pharisees and Sadducees? (Matthew 22:41)
2. Why did King David make a distinction between the two Names of God? (YHVH and Adonai)
3. Why is Hebrews Chapter One important to understanding and interpreting Psalm 110:1? How does Hebrews Chapter One answer Jesus' question in Matthew 22:41?
4. What happens when we say "yes" to Jesus?

Lesson 5

Isaiah Chapter 1
Foreshadow of the Savior

Isaiah ministered for a little over 40 years (740-697 B.C.). During this time four Judean kings reigned. They were Uzziah, Jotham, Ahaz, and Hezekiah.

Isaiah wrote during a time of prosperity much like the prosperity that the United States has experienced since its founding. However, the writings of Isaiah, and other prophets contemporary to him, reveal that people were spiritually destitute. Here in America, being at the pinnacle of power and prosperity, we today would pay little attention to a person who was forecasting our demise as a country if we do not turn from our wicked ways. These were the conditions in which Isaiah was giving his prophetic messages.

The main theme of the book of Isaiah is about salvation and the coming of the Savior. The Name of Jesus in Hebrew, *Yeshua*, means "Yahweh saves" or "salvation." The angel told Joseph in Matthew 1:21: *"She will give birth to a Son and you are to give Him the Name Jesus* (Yeshua)*, because He will **save** His people from their sins."* Jesus is just the English way of saying Yeshua. Later, we will look deeper into the root meaning of the Hebrew words translated salvation.

This study is not intended to be a verse by verse exposition, but is intended to show the many ways Isaiah was shown Jesus and His glory; and the ensuing prophetic implications in history, salvation and judgment of what Isaiah saw.

Isaiah starts his book with a vision concerning Judah and Jerusalem. When David was king, he was king over the twelve tribes of Israel. It was the whole nation of Israel. When King David's son, Solomon, became king, in order to build the temple and his palace, Solomon placed a heavy taxation burden on the people. They were taxed almost to the breaking point. When Solomon's son Rehoboam became king after his father's death (in 930 B.C.), he was advised to go easy on the people because of the heavy burden his father placed on them. Rehoboam rejected this advice and taxed them even more. As a result, the northern ten tribes seceded from the union of twelve tribes and became a separate nation known as Israel, with Samaria as its capital. The southern two tribes of Judah and Benjamin became a nation known as Judah, with Jerusalem as its capital. Some years later there was a war between the two, but for the most part there was an uneasy peace between them.

When Isaiah spoke the prophetic Word of God, some of it was directed to the northern ten tribes of Israel, but by and large Isaiah prophesied to the southern kingdom of Judah. Tradition tells us that Rome was being founded at about the same time. This becomes significant for a couple of reasons. As you know, Rome later became the center of power of the Roman Empire. By the time of Jesus' earthly ministry, the Roman Empire ruled all of the then known earth. The Romans' unique form of capital punishment—being nailed to a cross—was reserved for non-Roman citizens. King David, speaking of the Savior in Psalm 22, foresees the piercing of Jesus' hands and feet 1,000 years before it happened. Isaiah says in Chapter 53 that *"He was pierced for our transgressions."* That could include not only His hands and feet, but also a spear in His side. This kind of prophetic accuracy cannot be the result of a guess. It had to be divinely given.

Knowledge and Understanding Critical

When God starts speaking to the southern kingdom of Judah through Isaiah, He brings up this fact in Isaiah 1:2: *"...I reared children and brought them* (Israel) *up, but they have rebelled against Me. The ox knows his master, the donkey his owner's manger, but Israel does not **know**, My people do not **understand**.*" The reference here to not knowing and understanding concerns not knowing and understanding God and His requirements. That may not sound like much, but it was a serious problem for the Israelites. Hosea, Isaiah's contemporary, spoke of this problem in his book in Chapter 3, verse 6: *"My people are destroyed from lack of **knowledge**."* Again, at the end of verse 14: *"A people without **understanding** will come to ruin."* It was important for the people to whom Isaiah was speaking to have an accurate knowledge and understanding of God and His Word. It is just as important for us to have an accurate knowledge and understanding of God. There are consequences if we don't.

The Holy One of God

The last sentence of Isaiah 1:4 indicates why the people of Judah did not have accurate knowledge and understanding. Isaiah says: *"They have forsaken the **LORD**; they have spurned the **Holy One of Israel** and turned their backs on Him."* Now, we know this rendering of **LORD** is translated directly from Yahweh and refers to the Father, but is the "Holy One of Israel" one and the same as "LORD"? In Psalm 16:9 and 10, King David, speaking about the Holy One that was to come, says this: *"Therefore my heart is glad and my tongue rejoices; my body also will rest secure, because You will not abandon me to the grave, nor will You let Your **Holy One** see decay."* The Apostle Luke, confirming this Psalm was about Jesus, writes in Acts 2:29-32: *"Brothers, I can tell you confidently that the patriarch David died and was buried, and his tomb is here to this day. But he was a prophet and knew that God had promised him on oath that He would place one of his descendants on his throne. Seeing what was ahead, he spoke of the resurrection of the Christ, that He was not abandoned to the grave, nor did His body see decay. God has raised this Jesus to life, and we are all witnesses of the fact."*

In Luke 4:34, Jesus encounters a demon. This evil spirit cried at the top of his voice *"Ha! What do you want with us, Jesus of Nazareth? Have You come to destroy us? I know who You are—the **Holy One of God**."* In

John 6:69, Peter says to Jesus, *"We believe and know that You are the **Holy One of God.***"

Twice in the Old Testament and three times in the New Testament, we have a positive identification of the "Holy One of God." The Holy One of God, and the Holy One of Israel, whose body did not see decay, are one and the same. It is Yeshua, Jesus. Therefore, we could render the last sentence of Isaiah 1:4 this way: *"They have forsaken God the Father and they have spurned Yeshua* [Jesus) *and turned their backs on Him."* That is why the Israelites lacked accurate knowledge of God.

When we tell the Triune God to buzz off, to get out of our lives, and turn our backs on Him, saying that our way is better, He will allow us to stumble. He will allow us to eat with the hogs, as the prodigal son did, until we come to our senses and return to Him. Have you eaten with the hogs? What kind of mud pit have you wallowed in before you came to your senses about God?

If you have been there, you can help others get out. Ask yourself this question: When have you grown the most spiritually, when times were good or when times were rough? Everyone will say when times were rough. So the key to having the rough times go a little more smoothly for you, spiritually speaking, is to read and study the Bible and grow spiritually when times are good.

The Law is Important

Beginning in Isaiah 1:10 and continuing through verse 23, God begins itemizing the Jewish people's insincere worship practices and willful moral disobedience to Him. Verse 10 begins: *"Hear the Word of the **LORD**, you rulers of Sodom; listen to the law of our God, you people of Gomorrah!"* Why was this command to listen to the law of God important? There are, no doubt, many answers we can give here but Galatians 3:24 says it best: *"So the law was put in charge to lead us to Christ that we might be justified by faith."* How could these people be eventually lead to Christ or recognize Him when He comes if they didn't listen to and follow the law?

The truth is, they didn't listen to the law or the prophets, and they didn't recognize Christ when He came. Luke 19:41-44 bears out this lack of recognition: *"As He approached Jerusalem and saw the city, He wept over it and said 'If you, even you, had only known on this day what would bring you peace, but now it is hidden from your eyes. The days will come upon you when your enemies will build an embankment against you and encircle you and hem you in on every side. They will dash you to the ground, you and the children within your walls. They will not leave one stone on another, **because you did not recognize the time of God's coming to you.**'"* This prophecy was fulfilled forty years after Jesus spoke these words, when Titus, the Roman general, destroyed the city and the temple in 70 A.D.

Do you see that? These terrible things happened to them because they did not recognize the time of God's coming to them. They did not recognize it because they did not study and listen to the Word of God. Will people today miss out on the glorious Rapture and participation in the Second Coming of Christ for the same reasons?

The other thing Isaiah 1:10 does, is refer to the people of Judah and Jerusalem as rulers and people of Sodom and Gomorrah. One of the moral traits of Sodom and Gomorrah was that they gave themselves up to sexual immorality and perversion (Jude 1:7). Isaiah 1:21 says: *"Now the city of Jerusalem was full of murderers."* This was a condition that was also prevalent during the days of Noah. God said that the earth was corrupted in His sight and full of violence. God said: *"I'm going to put an end to all people, for the earth is filled with violence."* (Genesis 6:11) So, when God compares Judah and Jerusalem to Sodom and Gomorrah, we know that the people were practicing sexual immorality and perversion, along with being extremely violent and corrupt. This type of behavior is the natural outcome of people who do not listen to and follow the law of God. They acted as though there was no God. As the last verse in the book of Judges indicates, *"...every Israelite did as he saw fit."* In other words, *"...every man did that which was right in their own eyes."* (KJV) Their concept of right and wrong was based on their own individual concept of what was right and wrong, and this concept would change as circumstances changed. It was not based on God's law. They were setting themselves up for suffering and judgment.

Our Daily Actions Count

In Isaiah 1:11, God very clearly lays out His disgust with the multitude of sacrifices that have no meaning to Him. He commands them to stop bringing meaningless offerings. He hates their new moon festivals and appointed feasts. God says even if the Israelites offered many prayers, He would not listen, because their hands were full of blood. In verse 16, He commands them to *"Stop doing wrong, and learn to do right. Seek justice, encourage the oppressed, defend the cause of the fatherless, plead the case of the widow."* God is saying here that just because these people are going through religious practices and praying to Him, that He would not accept their outward religious ceremony and prayers, because their hearts and the practices of their daily lives were not right with Him.

What message does this hold for us in the Church today? Could it be our worship, praise and prayers on Sunday are meaningless because of the way we live and conduct ourselves the other six days of the week? Do we, as Christians, walk our talk? The larger the gap between our walk and our talk, the less effective we will be in winning souls to the kingdom of God. Nobody is perfect, and we do live in the era of saving grace, but that does not give us a license to sin (Jude 1:4). This sinful behavior was not acceptable to God during Isaiah's time, and it is not acceptable Christian behavior in this, the Church Age.

The Apostle Paul is just as clear when he writes in I Corinthians 6:9-11: *"Do you not know that the wicked will not inherit the kingdom of God? Do not be deceived: neither the sexually immoral nor idolaters nor adulterers nor male prostitutes nor homosexual offenders nor thieves nor the greedy nor drunkards nor slanderers nor swindlers will inherit the kingdom of God."* Period. You cannot attend church every Sunday, sing in the choir, teach Sunday school or anything else and expect to go to heaven, if you practice any of the above lifestyles on a continuing basis. The Apostle Paul says you will not inherit the kingdom of God. This is not to imply salvation by works; even if you live a good moral life and do these good works, salvation still only comes through the shed blood of Jesus Christ. Paul does go on to say in verse 11: *"And that is what some of you **were**. But you were washed, you were **sanctified**, you were **justified** in the name of the Lord Jesus Christ and by the Spirit of our God."* This indicates we can repent of our previous lifestyle, turn our backs on, and walk away from, our practice of sin, and invite Jesus to be our Lord and Savior.

It seems as though some use the term "Lord and Savior" rather loosely. They invite the Lord in as Savior, but do not act or live as though He is Lord of their lives. The word "Lord" carries with it the connotation of ownership, of ruler. When we invite the Lord into our heart and lives, we are making Him our ruler, someone whom we agree to let rule our lives. We also transfer ownership from ourselves to the Lord. We are no longer our own but His, allowing Him to use us as He pleases. When we truly invite Jesus to be our Lord and Savior, then we become washed in His sacrificial blood. We become sanctified and justified. To be "sanctified" means to be <u>made</u> holy, to be set apart for the work of God. "Justified" is one of those churchy words that simply means "just as though you have not sinned." Your slate has been wiped clean. We all have a past, some worse than others, but Jesus will wipe it clean if you let Him. From today on you can start all over again. You can have a new beginning. It is not often you can go back and start all over again in this life, but you can with God. If you have not yet started your new beginning with God, why not start now? Just ask Him.

Faith Questions

1. Why was it important for the Israelites to listen to the Law that God gave Moses?
2. What does Galations 3:24 say was the ultimate purpose for the Law?
3. Why is faith without works dead? (James 2:14-22)
4. How can claiming Jesus as Lord and Savior be misused?

Lesson 6

Isaiah Chapters 2 Through 4
In the Last Days

Isaiah 2:2 begins this way: *"In the last days."* This verse is pretty direct. It leaves little doubt as to the time frame it is talking about. Many believe "the last days" started when Israel became a nation in 1948. From God's perspective, it could have started well before this date, and it seems to continue well into the Millennial reign of Christ. What follows is Isaiah talking about the conditions and future historical account of events that occur sometime during that time period.

Isaiah uses key phrases (as do the other prophets) that subtly indicate the "last days." As examples, you may see the phrases "in that day," "at that time," "day of the LORD." You can be sure when you see these phrases (and you should train yourself to look for them), that they will almost always refer to the "end times," the last days. These phrases stand as flags to catch and direct our attention to a specific time (the end times) and events surrounding that time.

Now, some people may say that these phrases just refer to God's judgment, like what befell the Israelites during the Babylonian captivity, or when Rome destroyed Jerusalem and the temple in 70 A.D., and that would be correct; these phrases do refer to those things. However, when you consider the nature of dual prophecies, where the prophecy can refer to more than one time period, then you have to consider: Does this, or could this, have ramifications for the last days? Most of the time, it will. Chapter 2 specifically targets the last days, and the first five verses seem to be specifically speaking of a time early in the Millennial reign of Christ.

The Light Identified

Let's concentrate on Isaiah 2:5 for a minute. *"Come, O house of Jacob, let us walk in the **Light** of the* LORD.*"* Here, the word light is highlighted, because Isaiah (as well as the New Testament) has much to teach us about this Light.

Consider for a moment that you are an electronic engineer. You have your competitor's computer in front of you. It is fast, has a lot of storage, and generally is a better product for the money than what your company offers. You want to know what makes it tick. So you take the cover off, and begin what is known in the trade as "reverse engineering," examining every part, diode, and integrated circuit that makes the final product what it is.

We will use this same process concerning **light**, and start with Jesus and what He says about Himself in John 8:12. *"When Jesus spoke again to the people, He said, 'I am the **Light** of the world. Whoever follows Me will never walk in darkness, but will have the **Light** of life.'"*

John tells us in Chapter 7 that Jesus went to the Feast of Tabernacles. He taught in the temple courts. In verse 37, Jesus told His listeners: *"'If a man is thirsty, let him come to Me and drink. Whoever believes in Me, as the Scripture has said, streams of living water will flow from within him.' By this He meant the Spirit, whom those who believe in Him were later to receive."*

One of the customs of the Feast of Tabernacles was to light four very immense lamps. These lamps stood on top of two columns estimated to be around 70 feet high. Each lamp held about 20 gallons of oil. The robes of the priests were used as wicks. When these lamps were lit on the evening of the first day of the Feast, it was said that they not only lit up the Court of the Women, but that there was not a place in the whole of Jerusalem that was not illuminated by them. The reason for this custom was to simulate the pillar of fire and cloud that accompanied the Israelites during their sojourn in the desert. Therefore, Jesus could point to this column of light with its smoky, cloud-like appearance given off by the burning oil, and by inference claim this custom was in reality a representation of Him and His presence. (Refer to the teaching on Angel of God in Exodus 14:19-20.) This is the backdrop on which Jesus stated that He was the **Light** of the world. The people He was teaching would have understood exactly what Jesus was saying about Himself. In fact, as Jesus continues in Chapter 8 explaining and implying His deity, His teaching was so repugnant to them that they picked up stones to stone Him by the end of the chapter.

Isaiah refers to walking in the **Light** in 2:5, and again in 9:2: *"The people walking in darkness have seen a great* **Light***; on those living in the land of the shadow of death the* **Light** *has dawned."* The church has historically pointed to these verses in 9:1-7 as a direct prophecy concerning Christ. (We will discuss Isaiah 9:1-7 in more detail later.) It is clear that the **Light** seen by those walking in darkness is none other than Yeshua, Christ the Messiah. (The Greek *Messiah* and Hebrew *Maschiach* both mean "Anointed One.") Isaiah further identifies this **Light** in 10:17 as the **Holy One**: *"The* **Light of Israel** *will become a fire, their* **Holy One** *a flame."* Isaiah 49:1 is speaking of Jesus, and Isaiah further states in verse 6b that: *"God will also make You* (Jesus) *a* **Light** *for the Gentiles, that You may bring My salvation to the ends of the earth."* When you add all of these little identifications together, we start to see the bigger picture as Isaiah knew it and as Jesus knew it…that He was and is the **Light** of the world.

Is He the **Light** in your world? You can make it so, if you want to.

Trying to Escape

As Isaiah goes on in Chapter 2, verse 6, to the end of Chapter 2, he continues to describe the conditions that will be prevalent in the last days. Verses 10 and 19 are especially noteworthy, for Isaiah describes men going into caves, hiding under rocks and going into holes in the ground, trying to escape from the dread of the LORD. The only other time in history that the Bible speaks of this phenomenon is at the beginning of the Tribulation period, as recorded in Revelation 6:15-17: *"Then the kings of the earth, the princes, the generals, the rich, the mighty, and every slave and every free man hid in caves and among the rocks of the mountains. They called to the mountains and the rocks, 'Fall on us and hide us from the face of Him who sits on the throne and from the wrath of the Lamb! For the great day of their wrath has come, and who can stand?'"*

Have you been following along in your Bible? It is important that you do. That way you can ensure nothing is taken out of context. Cults love to take Scripture out of context, to help create non-Biblical, perverted theologies to which they hold.

In Chapter 2, Isaiah uses the phrase "in that day" to indicate the last days. In Chapter 3 he uses the same phrase in verse 18 to describe what will happen in some time period other than the last days. This could be a prophecy concerning the Babylonian invasion, or the Roman destruction of Jerusalem and its temple; the event that Isaiah describes could apply to either.

The Branch

As we go into Chapter 4, Isaiah is again describing end times. (The definition of "end times" for this study will generally mean the seven-year Tribulation period, and the very beginning of the Millennial reign of Christ.) Verse 2 begins: *"In that day the **Branch** of the LORD will be beautiful and glorious...."* Who or what is this **Branch**? Isaiah, Jeremiah, and Zechariah all speak of this Branch, and in all cases, record that the Branch has deistic qualities. Let's review some other Scriptures so we can be more certain of the identity of this Branch. Isaiah speaks of the Branch again in 11:1-2: *"For a shoot will come up from the stump of Jesse; from his roots a **Branch** will bear fruit. The Spirit of the LORD will rest on Him; the Spirit of wisdom and of understanding, the Spirit of counsel and of power, the Spirit of knowledge and of the fear of the LORD, and He will delight in the fear of the LORD."*

Jesse was the father of King David. So the Branch will be of the lineage of King David. That means Isaiah is talking about a human. This human being has special qualities that no other human being possesses or has ever possessed. First of all, the Holy Spirit is giving Him full wisdom and understanding of counsel, and power, and knowledge of the LORD. Colossians 1:19 indicates that *"God was pleased to have all His fullness dwell in Him* (Jesus).*"* Jeremiah 23:5 says: *"'The days are coming,' declares the* LORD, *'when I will raise up to David a righteous* **Branch***, a King who will reign wisely and do what is just and right in the land. In His days Judah will be saved and Israel will live in safety. This is the Name by which He will be called:* **the LORD our Righteousness.** *'"*

The prophet Zechariah records in Chapter 6:12-13 that this Branch will build the temple, will sit and rule on His throne as King, and He will also be a Priest on His throne. *"And there will be harmony between the two."* Now we know the Branch is also going to be Priest, as well as King. The writer of Hebrews also informs us that Jesus fulfills the role of great High Priest. Hebrews 4:14-15 says: *"Therefore, since we have a great High Priest who has gone through the heavens, Jesus the Son of God, let us hold firmly to the faith we profess. For we do not have a High Priest who is unable to sympathize with our weakness, but we have one who has been tempted in every way, just as we are, yet was without sin."*

In Jeremiah 33:15, Jeremiah gives a description very similar to Jeremiah 23:5 that was quoted above. There is only one person who can be Priest and King, endowed with the fullness of God through the Holy Spirit, and come from the lineage of King David: the God-man Yeshua, Jesus. He is the **Branch**!

Let's review the names and titles that we have discovered so far that identify Yeshua, Jesus. He is the Glory of the LORD, the Angel of the LORD. the Angel of God. He is Adonai – Lord; the Holy One of God, the Holy One of Israel, the Holy One. He is the Light of the LORD, the Light of the world, the Light of life. He is the Branch, High Priest, King, and the LORD our Righteousness.

Is the Lord Jesus the Light of life to you? Is He Lord? Is He the Holy One? Is the Lord Jesus any of these to you? Isaiah has more names and titles yet to be discovered. As previously stated, Isaiah saw Jesus' glory and wrote about Him. The Apostle John wasn't kidding when he made the statement: *"Isaiah said this because he saw Jesus' glory and spoke about Him."* (John 12:41).

Faith Questions

1. How was it significant for Jesus to identify with the column of light?
2. Why is it important to compare Scripture with other, similar Scripture?
3. What traits does the Branch possess?
4. Who is the "high priest" spoken of in Hebrews 4:14-15?
5. What trait was God pleased to have dwelling in Jesus?

Lesson 7

Isaiah Chapters 5 Through 7
What More Could He Do?

God is lamenting in Isaiah Chapter 5 about how He has done everything He could to bring the people of Judah and Jerusalem along in a manner worthy of Him. He compares them to a vineyard. The vineyard was planted in fertile ground. He cleared the stones, pruned the vines and did everything possible to make the conditions right for a plentiful harvest. But this effort only produced bad grapes. The people of Judah and Jerusalem were so preoccupied with their daily lives, with their pursuit of wealth, and the nurturing of their perverted, self-gratifying social lives, that *"They [had] no regard for the deeds of the* LORD, *no respect for the work of His hands."* (5:12b) God gives us our free will. This "having no regard for the LORD," or not caring about people in general, is what happens when strong-willed, rebellious people reject God: they were "bad grapes." *"Therefore, My people will go into exile for lack of understanding."* (5:13)

Isaiah again raises the issue of this lack of understanding, as he did in Chapter 2. It was a grievous offense in the eyes of God. We should heed the warning as well. For the people of Judah and Jerusalem, it caused them to go into exile in Babylon.

Scoffing at God's Word

In verse 19 God is responding to those who say: *"Let God hurry, let Him hasten His work so we may see it. Let it approach, let the plan of the Holy One of Israel* (Jesus) *come so we may know it."* The people were saying this in a very scoffing, condescending way. It was like a dare to God, and was an extension of their disregard for the Word of God. But they were not the only ones guilty of this type of sin. II Peter 3:3-4 says: *"First of all, you must understand that in the last days scoffers will come, scoffing and following their evil desires. They will say, 'Where is this coming He promised? Ever since our fathers died, everything goes on as it has since the beginning of creation.'"*

Well, we are in the last days, and the beat goes on! People are scoffing today, denying the Word of God. They ridicule those of us who call Jesus Lord. They call us intolerant. They fail to understand that we worship an intolerant God. He is intolerant of sin. When we tell them what God says is sinful, they call us hateful. Their very speech, their labeling of Christians as intolerant, their ridicule of our moral positions and stances, their persecutions of us, even killing us because we are Christians, all reflect the signs of our times…the end times!

As Isaiah says in 5:20: *"Woe to those who call evil good and good evil, who put darkness for light and light for darkness, who put bitter for sweet and sweet for bitter."* This redefining of right and wrong, good and bad, exchanging healthy behavior for unhealthy, provides the foundational basis that allows situational ethics to come into vogue. The world can then frame the ethical and moral arguments in their favor. This allows God to be redefined. This redefinition of God runs the full range of transforming God into something He is not, or eliminating Him altogether. God, too, then becomes situational… becoming anything people want Him to be, or not be, at any particular time. The end product, then, is that God is no longer God as He is revealed in the Bible. This is the current view of the world, and this view is in conflict with the God of the Bible and people who put their faith in Him. Satan has this world turned upside down. His time is short and he is seeking to devour whom he may. (I Peter 5:8) Satan has gorged himself well. The Christian worldview is definitely a hated minority view in the world today.

The world thinks: *"[They] are wise in their own eyes and clever in their own sight"* (Isaiah 5:21), but they do not **know,** they do not **understand,** *"they have rejected the law of the LORD Almighty and spurned the Word of the Holy One of Israel. Therefore the LORD's anger burns against this people."* (Isaiah 5:24b-25a)

Stand Firm in Your Faith

There is a widely-circulated old saying that "If you don't stand for something you'll fall for anything." It had a profound effect on many people, encouraging them to have backbone on issues important to them. Isaiah 7:9b says something similar, but is more specific to the issue of faith: *"If you do not stand firm in your faith, you will not stand at all."* This is profound. It is critical, and the admonition is given over and over in the New Testament. Matthew 10:22 says: *"All men will hate you because of Me, but he who stands firm to the end will be saved."* I Corinthians 16:13: *"Be on your guard; stand firm in the faith; be men of courage; be strong."* II Thessalonians 2:15: *"So then, brothers, stand firm and hold to the teachings...."* I Peter 5:8-9a: *"Be self-controlled and alert. Your enemy the devil prowls around like a roaring lion looking for someone to devour. Resist him, standing firm in the faith...."*

These are just a few of many verses that echo Isaiah's admonition to stand firm in your faith. But how can we do this? How can we best stand firm in our faith? Certainly, putting on the armor of God as found in Ephesians 6:10-18, is a good place to start. But even more basic to this is Romans 10:17: *"Consequently, faith comes from hearing the message, and the message is heard through the Word of Christ."* If your faith is weak, get into the Word. If your faith has been shaken, get into the Word. If you want to increase your faith, get into the Word. This was the Apostle Paul's teaching to the Romans.

The Virgin Birth

The next important event in Isaiah 7 is the prophetic promise of the virgin birth found in verse 14: *"Therefore the Lord Himself will give you a sign: the virgin will be with child and will give birth to a Son and will call Him Immanuel."* This is an important verse, so let's take the time to scrutinize the words, teachings and implications it has to offer. The Church has always ascribed this prophecy to the virgin birth of Jesus the Messiah. In order to do that, it seems as though this verse would have had to be taken out of context. Based on the verses following verse 14, this verse is clearly speaking of an event in history in which Isaiah was a participant.

But knowing that prophecy can have two or more time references for fulfillment, we must look for other historical or Scriptural verification. The Apostle Matthew, explaining the events surrounding the birth of Jesus Christ, and teaching with the power and authority of Jesus Himself, specifically points out in verses 22 and 23 of Chapter 1 that, indeed, Isaiah 7:14 is a direct prophecy concerning the birth of Jesus. *"All this took place to fulfill what the Lord had said through the prophet: the virgin will be with child and will give birth to a Son, and they will call Him Immanuel, which means 'God with us.'"*

Now let's go back to Isaiah 7:14, *"The* **Lord** *Himself will give you a sign."* Take notice of the capitalization of the highlighted "Lord." Jesus Himself will give you a sign. What is a sign? Something supernatural? Something beyond the probability of chance happening? Something that occurs that has no explanation in physics? Something that occurs which is otherwise impossible? Yes, all of these, and so much more. The sign will be that a virgin will give birth. Technically, the Hebrew word translated "virgin" could mean a young woman, as well as a young woman who has never had sexual relations with a man. Let's consider the culture that surrounded Mary and Joseph. At the time of Mary and Joseph, marriages were arranged. There was no courtship, no dating, no relationship based on love. It was strictly a contract offer to the family of the potential bride, and she had the right to reject the offer. There was a strict separation of young people, coupled with the religious law of stoning for adultery and infidelity. Mary herself expressed her incredulousness regarding how she was going to become pregnant since she was a virgin, never having been with a man. (Luke 1:34) You can be sure that Mary was a true virgin.

A "virgin giving birth" is a conflict of terms. It would have been impossible for a virgin in Mary's day to give birth. The very act that causes conception takes away the virginity. Therefore, a virgin can't give birth. Since it is impossible for a true virgin to give birth, therein lies the sign: the supernatural, the happening that has no explanation in physics—Mary's pregnancy occurred without interaction with the human male counterpart, and resulted in the humanly-impossible virgin birth of Immanuel ("God with us").

John 1:1 states: *"In the beginning was the Word, and the Word was with God, and the Word was God."* In algebra, if A=B then B=A. If the Word is God, then God is the Word. John 1:14 says: *"The Word* [God] *became flesh and lived for a while among us* (Immanuel)." God in human flesh was the greatest **Sign** of all, and Jesus is the one who fulfilled the sign for us.

Faith Questions

1. Why do people scoff at God's Word?
2. What is the problem with weak faith?
3. How is a "virgin birth" different from a "normal birth?"

Lesson 8

Isaiah Chapters 8 and 9
God Controls the Historical and Spiritual Outcomes

When Isaiah began prophesying and it was yet early in his prophetic career, the Assyrian empire had not yet come across its borders to become a world power. Here in Chapter 8, Isaiah prophesies that in the near future the king of Assyria would carry Damascus and Samaria off into captivity. In verses 7 and 8, the king of Assyria and his army are depicted as the floodwaters of a mighty river sweeping over all the northern 10 tribes of Israel *"and sweep[ing] on into Judah, swirling over it, passing through it and reaching up to the neck."*

What does this mean, the king of Assyria sweeping on into Judah, swirling over it, passing through it and reaching up to the neck? For the moment let's turn to II Kings Chapter 18. Picking up the commentary that starts at verse 17, we see that *"The king of Assyria sent his supreme commander, his chief officer and his field commander with a large army from Lachish to King Hezekiah at Jerusalem. They came up to Jerusalem and stopped at the aqueduct of the Upper Pool...."*

We can now see Isaiah's prophecy being fulfilled with the Assyrian army just outside the walls of Jerusalem. Jerusalem is the neck, but they came no further. Hezekiah contacted Isaiah to inquire of the Lord what he as king should do. Isaiah inquired of the Lord, King Hezekiah prayed, and the answer came back in II Kings 19:10 that Jerusalem would not be handed over to the king of Assyria. How can this be? Assyria had an absolutely overwhelming force surrounding Jerusalem. How could Isaiah's word be trusted when King Hezekiah did not possess the physical means to resist?

It certainly would be easy at this point to walk by sight and not by faith. Walking by sight is the natural thing to do. It is what most of us do when faced with a mountain of a crisis. We can't see through the mountain and we can't see around the mountain. We don't even begin to have the energy to climb it. We can't see through the storm or know what the storm will bring, or have the courage to endure it. Jesus can, and He has the solution. Walking by faith, then, is trusting Jesus... trusting Jesus to provide the answer, to solve the problem, to make the problem go away, or trusting and knowing that Jesus will walk with you and beside you as you face your storm or mountain to give you courage and strength and direction.

Hezekiah was a good king. Hezekiah walked by faith and not by sight. "*Hezekiah trusted in the* LORD, *the God of Israel. There was no one like him among all the kings of Judah, either before him or after him,*" according to II Kings 18:5. In good times or in bad, nothing compares to having a godly king (or president) at the helm. (Read II Kings 18 and 19 for a more detailed account.)

The historical account showing that God is a God of His word, a God that keeps His promises, continues in II Kings 19:35. "*That night* **the Angel of the** LORD *went out and put to death 185,000 men in the Assyrian camp.*" That made the odds of a fair fight a little better. It vastly tilted the balance of power in favor of Hezekiah. Hezekiah and God comprised an army that nobody could defeat. "*When the people got up the next morning there were all these dead bodies! So Sennacherib King of Assyria broke camp and withdrew. He returned to Nineveh and stayed there.*" (II Kings 19:35b-36)

On the excavated walls of Nineveh are relief sculptures of all the conquered enemies of this Assyrian king being dragged back, naked and bleeding, in humiliation and defeat. These kings always tout and puff up their victories but never mention their defeats. But of King Hezekiah the wall says this: "The king of Assyria had Hezekiah pinned

God Controls the Historical and Spiritual Outcomes

up like a bird in a cage." What better proof of the historical event, and its outcome, than this!

Going back to Isaiah 8:8, Isaiah finishes the verse with *"O **Immanuel**! [God is with us!]"* He is indeed with us. He promises never to forsake us or leave us. He was with Israel then and protected them. He is with Israel today and protects them. During the Tribulation period, when the nations will once again swirl over Israel going right up to the neck, God will once again protect and save Jerusalem by destroying the armies and the nations that come against her. It historically happened once. No one should doubt that it won't happen again, just as the prophets predict. **The Angel of the LORD** (the pre-incarnate Jesus) destroyed the army coming against Jerusalem in Hezekiah's day and Jesus will do it again at His Second Coming!

This leads us naturally into verses 9 and 10. *"Raise the war cry, you nations, and be shattered! Listen, all you distant lands. Prepare for battle, and be shattered! Prepare for the battle, and be shattered! Devise your strategy, but it will be thwarted; propose your plan, but it will not stand, for **God is with us**."*

The king of Assyria devised his strategy but it was thwarted. Even today many nations of the Middle East have come against Israel. In 1948 the Arab Middle East made plans to drive Israel, the new state of Israel, into the sea. They made their plans and devised their strategies, and they were not only thwarted, but shattered. In 1967 the nations of the Arab Middle East came against Israel, which became known as the Six-Day War. Again their strategies and plans were thwarted and their armies shattered. In 1973 the same thing happened again, with the same outcome.

Israel was, and is, *"the apple of God's eye"* (Zechariah 2:8). If you touch God's sensitive eye, He will react. At the end of the Tribulation period, when **all** nations propose their plans and devise their strategies to come against Israel, they will again be thwarted by the Second Coming of Jesus Christ. (Zechariah 12:3, 14:3)

Satan, Israel's Ultimate Enemy

What does all this mean? The nations have tried to destroy Israel since Jacob was first given the name of Israel by God. And the conflict even goes back beyond that. The root lies in the age-old struggle of good versus evil; the struggle between Satan and God. From the beginning, Satan has tried to disrupt and destroy the things of God. God's purpose goes back to the Garden of Eden in Genesis 3:15, where God said He was going to put an enmity between Satan and Eve, between his offspring and hers. God said to the serpent: "*He will crush your head and you will strike His heel.*" This comparison between the offspring of Satan versus the offspring of Eve is very unusual in Scripture. This seed, or offspring as it is sometimes translated, only comes through the males. God promised Abraham that his seed ("offspring") would be a blessing to the nations.

In other places the Bible talks about the seed of David. But in Genesis 3:15, the offspring of the woman, Eve, and by default Mary, will be at odds with Satan and his offspring. This is a prophetic promise, the first of its kind, showing the outcome of the battle between Satan and the Son of God, Jesus. Jesus will crush Satan's head, which will be a fatal blow. The tools of Satan that keep people in bondage to sin, to fear (like the fear of death, in bondage to loneliness and to addictions of all kinds), will receive a fatal blow. This prophecy has not yet been totally fulfilled. But through the power of the resurrected Christ and the indwelling of His Holy Spirit, we can have victory over these things now. However, the rest of humankind will remain in bondage until Satan is taken out of the way.

In the meantime, from the time of Genesis until now and on into the future, Satan will continue to try to destroy the things of God. How does God allow Satan to accomplish these things? We get some idea of this from the book of Job, Chapters 1 and 2. According to these chapters in Job, Satan can use people, groups of people, tribes and nations, as well as what we call "natural events," and also health problems.

After God gave Satan permission to test Job, the first thing that happened was the Sabeans attacked and killed Job's family. Satan didn't kill Job's family; the Sabeans did. Then fire fell from the sky, the Chaldeans formed three raiding parties, and a mighty wind swept in from the desert. And finally Satan used Job's wife. His wife said to him, "*Are you still holding on to your integrity? Curse God and die!*" (Job 2:9)

God Controls the Historical and Spiritual Outcomes

The Bible doesn't say that Satan had his hand in every one of of these events personally. He just found unrepentant, unregenerate, unbelieving human beings to do his dirty work for him. Getting these kinds of people to do his dirty work has always been easy for Satan. The best part for Satan is these people he is using do not even know they are being used. They are pawns of Satan. People today in the Middle East and all over the world are being used by Satan and they don't even know it. This is even happening in the "church," where some are trying to nullify the promises of God made to and through Israel. Satan has tried time after time to destroy the Jewish people and thus nullify the promises of God made through them. History is full of these attempts, and the Bible has example after example. In the book of Esther there is a man named Haman, a type of antichrist, who tries to destroy the Jewish people.

King Herod, another type of antichrist, upon hearing that the Messiah was born, dispatched his militia to kill all male children under two years of age (Matthew 2:16). Satan, as a matter of self-preservation, was trying to keep the seed of the woman (Jesus) from being born and surviving. In Revelation 12:4-5, we have a picture of Satan standing *"in front of the woman who was about to give birth, so that he might devour her Child the moment it was born. She gave birth to a Son, a male Child, Who will rule all the nations with an iron scepter. And her Child was snatched up to God and to His throne."* Revelation 12:17 speaks about the dragon, Satan, who was *"...enraged at the woman and went off to make war against the rest of her offspring; those who obey God's Commandments and hold to the testimony of Jesus."* Here again Satan is working behind the scenes getting human beings to do his work.

Today we see millions of people hating Israel and the Jewish people without cause. Even Hitler, another type of antichrist, thought he was going to accomplish his "final solution" to the Jewish problem by eliminating **all** of the Jewish people. If Hitler had won World War II and accomplished this egregious goal, then Satan would have won. We could throw the Bible into the trash can. The prophecies and promises would have been broken and worthless. God could not allow the Satanically-motivated Hitler to win that war, if for no other reason than to preserve the Jewish people and to maintain the honor, glory and integrity of His holy Name, and the prophetic promises concerning His chosen people contained in His holy, written Word.

It can be historically demonstrated, when Hitler began rounding up the Jews to put them in the death camps, that the advancement of his war machine simultaneously started grinding to a halt. Thereafter, Germany suffered defeat after defeat until it collapsed. This was not a coincidence.

As was demonstrated earlier, many nations (even in recent times) have tried to destroy Israel and the Jewish people. In the Tribulation period all nations will come against Israel but their plans and their strategies will be thwarted. Psalm 83:2 says it very eloquently: *"See how your enemies are astir, how your foes rear their heads. With cunning they conspire against your people; they plot against those you cherish. 'Come,' they say, 'let us destroy them as a nation, that the name of Israel be remembered no more.' With one mind they plot together; they form an alliance against you."* Is this not what is going on today, as well? Satan's final thrust to annul the prophetic promises is when he brings all the nations against Israel to annihilate the Jewish people once and for all, trying to destroy the city of Jerusalem and its temple.

Satan was the motivating force behind all of the attempts throughout all of history to destroy and eliminate the Jewish people. Satan is the motivating force behind the current conflicts in the Middle East. It is the conflict between God the Father, Son, and Holy Spirit, and Satan, who wants to be God, being played out here on earth. It will continue to be played out until Satan is finally and everlastingly thrown into the lake of burning sulfur.

"Raise the war cry, you nations, and be shattered! Listen, all you distant lands. Prepare for battle, and be shattered! Prepare for the battle, and be shattered! Devise your strategy, but it will be thwarted; propose your plan, but it will not stand, for God is with us." (Isaiah 8:9-10)

The replacement theologists cannot possibly be right about the prophecies not having any bearing on what is happening in the land of Israel today. Prophecy is being fulfilled literally before our very eyes. They run the risk of unwittingly playing into the hands of Satan.

From Genesis to Revelation, the demonstration of unity of thought, unity of the message, unity of prophecy, is taking place. Look for it!

God Controls the Historical and Spiritual Outcomes

As Isaiah Chapter 8 continues on, God is telling Isaiah in verses 12-13 *"…do not fear what the people fear, and do not dread it."* What was it the Israelites feared? What was it they dreaded? Well, we could itemize each of the fears, and it would indeed be a very long list, or we could just encapsulate them all and say they feared and dreaded just about everything except the Almighty God. God reminds Isaiah that *"The LORD Almighty is the One you are to regard as holy, He is the One you are to fear, He is the One you are to dread."* We, also, are to regard God Almighty as holy and fear Him, but do we? Does the world fear God and regard Him as holy? I'm sure you know the answer to that question.

The Stone That Causes Men to Stumble

In Isaiah 8:14-15, God says *"…but for both houses of Israel He will be a Stone that causes men to stumble and a Rock that makes men fall. And for the people of Jerusalem He will be a trap and a snare. Many of them will stumble; they will fall and be broken."* Here, Isaiah is getting a glimpse of the Savior again. In Chapter 28, God further explains and describes this "Stone." Verse 16: *"See, I lay a Stone in Zion, a tested Stone, a precious Cornerstone for a sure foundation; the one who trusts will never be dismayed."*

The building practices and techniques that were in use in ancient times are still in use today. When laying block, or as then, using stone, it was of utmost importance to get the corner straight and square. The cornerstone had to be perfectly square and set exactly at right angles with an intersecting wall. It just couldn't be any old stone. If everything wasn't just right concerning this cornerstone, then the whole building would end up out of square and in danger of collapsing. King David got this same glimpse of Jesus and wrote about it in Psalm 118. We visited Psalm 118 earlier in regard to the East Gate and the procession from the Mount of Olives to the temple that historically was, and is to come. This time we will focus on the stone in verse 22: *"The Stone the builders rejected has become the **Capstone**."* As all of you probably know, when building a stone archway, the capstone is the very last stone put in place at the very top of the arch. Without it the arch would collapse. It is what holds it together.

This particular Capstone, which we will soon show is a code word for Jesus, is the one the builders rejected. As the builders looked over this Capstone, they perceived it to be flawed; they felt it could not be the one that could be used to hold things together for all times. The builders (high priests, Sadducees, Pharisees, and others), tripped and stumbled over the very One they were searching for. The Apostle Paul says in Romans 9:32 that they (the Jews) stumbled over the stumbling Stone. They perceived Yeshua, Jesus, to be flawed. In their eyes He could not possibly be the promised Messiah. He didn't fit their mold.

We get confirmation of the identity of this Capstone, this Rock, from I Peter 2:4-8: *"As you come to Him, the **living Stone**—rejected by men but chosen by God and precious to Him—you also, like living stones, are being built into a spiritual house to be a holy priesthood, offering spiritual sacrifices acceptable to God through Jesus Christ. For in Scripture it says: 'See, I lay a Stone in Zion, a chosen and precious Cornerstone, and the one who trusts in Him will never be put to shame.' Now to you who believe, this Stone is precious. But to those who do not believe, 'The Stone the builders rejected has become the Capstone,' and, 'A Stone that causes men to stumble and a Rock that makes them fall.' They stumble because they disobey the message—which is also what they were destined for."*

Let's focus for a minute on what Peter tells us in 2:5. *"As you come to Him, the living Stone—rejected by men but chosen by God and precious to Him—you also, like living stones, are being built into a spiritual house to be a holy priesthood...."*

Peter tells us we are to be like living stones, emulating the Stone the builders rejected. That makes it very plain that we are to be like cornerstones, which allow spiritual things to be built straight and true, in our faith and life. We are to be like capstones which hold things together in faith and life. We are to be Christ-like, having the mind and attitude of Christ Jesus (I Corinthians 2:16, Philippians 2:5). There is also one other concept we might consider. In the book of Joshua after the Israelites had miraculously crossed the Jordan River, God gives Joshua a directive to have 12 men, one from each tribe, go out into the middle of the Jordan River and pick up a large stone. They were to bring these stones back to shore and set them in a pile to serve as a sign among them. God told them that in the future, when their children ask, "What do these stones

God Controls the Historical and Spiritual Outcomes

mean?" they should tell them of the great miracles that took place and how God intervened to see the Israelites safely into the promised land (paraphrased).

We are to live our lives as "living stone" Christians; to be a sign of the miraculous saving work that God has done in our lives. Our children and others should see us and know that we are different, that we display the fruit of the Spirit (love, joy, peace, patience, kindness, goodness, faithfulness, gentleness and self-control), which the unbelieving world does not show. As others watch us work and interact with people they may get curious enough to ask why and how we are different. They notice the "living stone" sign; the door is now open for witnessing and evangelism.

The Prophetic Promise of the Savior

While Isaiah Chapter 8 speaks of the Messiah as a Stone and a Rock that causes men to stumble, Isaiah Chapter 9 continues the description of the Messiah in more detail. It gives the geographical area where He will be born, some of His names and titles, and the extent of His rule. Let's look a little closer at some of the details.

In verse 1, Isaiah states: *"In the past He humbled the land of Zebulun and the land of Naphtali, but in the future He will honor Galilee of the Gentiles, by the way of the sea, along the Jordan."* Micah gets even more specific as to where the Messiah will be born in Micah 5:2: *"But you, Bethlehem Ephrathah, though you are small among the clans of Judah, out of you will come for Me One Who will be ruler over Israel, Whose origins are from old, from ancient times."* Here again, we have evidence that Jesus has been around since before the beginning of time. Some translations even say "from days of eternity." The point is that Jesus didn't just show up Christmas morning. He has been around since eternity, and He guided and protected the Israelite people when they needed it most.

Getting back to Isaiah Chapter 9, verse 6 tells us *"...the government will be upon His shoulders, and He will be called Wonderful Counselor, Mighty God, Everlasting Father, Prince of Peace. Of the increase of His government and peace there will be no end."* Luke's account agrees with this. He says in 1:32-33: *"He will be great and will be called the Son of the*

Most High. The Lord will give Him the throne of His father David, and He will reign over the house of Jacob forever; His kingdom will never end."

To the names and titles listed earlier that Isaiah has identified with Messiah, Jesus, we can now add: Capstone, precious Cornerstone, living Stone, Rock, Wonderful Counselor, Mighty God, Everlasting Father, Prince of Peace. All of these are code words used to identify the One Who was, Who is, and Who is to come, the Messiah, Jesus. This list will continue to grow.

Faith Questions

1. The Angel of the Lord slew 185,000 soldiers in defense of Jerusalem. When will He (Jesus) do it again?
2. Who is Israel's ultimate enemy? Why?
3. Why wouldn't God allow Hitler to win World War II?
4. Why was the Living Stone precious to God?
5. When did Jesus come into existence?

Lesson 9

Isaiah Chapter 10
The Return to
the Mighty God

When God takes down His hedge of protection, and allows other nations to exercise judgment upon His people Israel, those nations that do come in and kill, pillage, rape and destroy will themselves be subject to God's judgment. An example is the case of Assyria, when God allowed the Babylonian empire to later come in and do the same to Assyria that the Assyrians did to Israel. Isaiah Chapter 10, in part, speaks of this phenomenon. Chapter 10 is also meant to give hope. The remnant of people taken captive by the Assyrian king would someday be allowed to return.

Isaiah 10:21, though, is speaking of a different time, a different remnant. This remnant would return to the **Mighty God**. We just read in Chapter 9 that one of the titles of Jesus would be **Mighty God**. So this remnant is going to return to Yeshua, Jesus. There weren't enough people in Israel at the time of Jesus' ministry who knew and accepted Him as the Mighty God, for them to be considered a remnant. So this verse must be speaking of a yet future time. The Apostle Paul wrote to the Romans in Chapters 9, 10 and 11, and spoke of this future remnant, and how there is no difference between Jew and Gentile. Romans 10:9

says: *"That if you confess with your mouth, Jesus is Lord, and believe in your heart that God raised Him from the dead, you will be saved."*

The Jewish people, if they are to be grafted back in, must repent and acknowledge Jesus as the Messiah (Romans 11:11-22). Many Jewish people have become believers in Yeshua and many more, no doubt, will follow their lead before the Tribulation period begins. This will only be a partial fulfillment of prophecy. The prophet Zechariah, who is rich in tribulation and end-time prophecy, gives us a description of the Jews turning *en masse* to Yeshua, the Mighty God, for salvation. At the end of the Tribulation period, when Jesus Christ returns bodily to earth for the second time, Zechariah 12:10-11 records the scene. *"And I will pour out on the house of David and the inhabitants of Jerusalem the spirit of grace and supplication. They will look on Me, **the One they have pierced**, and they will **mourn** for Him as one mourns for an only child, and **grieve** bitterly for Him as one grieves for a first born son. On that day the weeping in Jerusalem will be great...."* Here we have *en masse* the weeping of repentance for what they have done to the One they have pierced. And so a remnant will be saved. The remnant of Jacob will return to the **Mighty God** just as Isaiah predicted. Revelation 1:7 confirms this "looking on the One they have pierced" scenario: *"Look, He is coming with the clouds, and every eye will see Him, **even those who pierced Him**; and all the peoples of the earth will mourn because of Him. So shall it be! Amen."*

Are you noticing the unity of message and thought? The unity of prophetic promises? They span centuries, even millennia, with several different authors, but the message is always the same. This kind of detailed continuity cannot happen by chance or guess, but only through divine revelation. II Peter 1:19-21 says it best: *"And we have the word of the prophets made more certain, and you will do well to pay attention to it, as to a light shining in a dark place, until the day dawns and the Morning Star rises in your hearts. Above all, you must understand that no prophecy of Scripture came about by the prophet's own interpretation. For prophecy never had its origin in the will of man, but men spoke from God as they were carried along by the Holy Spirit."*

As a side note, Zechariah was written some 500 years before Christ was born. He told us, as did King David and Isaiah, that the Messiah would be pierced. This piercing was not only visible to the doubting disciple Thomas, but will also be visible at His Second Coming and forever. These visible scars will serve as a testimony and as a reminder of His love and sacrifice for us, forever and throughout all eternity.

Faith Questions

1. When will the remnant of Israel return *en masse* to Jesus?
2. What will be the evidence of Israel's repentance?

Lesson 10

Isaiah Chapters 11 Through 13
Jesus, the Branch

Isaiah Chapter 11 is one of those chapters that have a lot of elements to it. In the main it speaks of Jesus, His attributes, His mission, His biological lineage, and the time frame of His earthly ministry that includes both the Cross and the Crown, the Sacrificial Lamb and the Lion. In other words, there are aspects of Jesus and His ministry attributable only to His First Coming and there are other aspects attributable only to His Second Coming.

Verse 1 begins this way: *"A shoot will come up from the stump of Jesse; from his roots a Branch will bear fruit."* Have you ever cut down a tree where the only thing left was a stump sticking up? Or maybe you cut off an unwanted bush at ground level. If you have, you probably felt that took care of the problem. End of tree, end of story. But the following spring, lo and behold, here come these sprouts bearing green leaves out of the old rotted stump. Jesse was the father of King David. God had promised King David that he would always have a descendant on his throne, if all of those descendants would obey and follow God's demands and decrees. (1 Kings 2:4) A study of Kings and Chronicles would soon show how far short King David's descendants would fall.

After the Babylonian captivity, there have been no legitimate, God-appointed kings in Israel, or legitimate thrones for them to sit on, even to the present time. King Herod, a type of Antichrist, was an illegitimate king, not in the lineage of King David. Herod was sitting on David's throne when Jesus came to earth the first time. The Antichrist, when he comes, will also be an illegitimate usurper of the throne, and he will proclaim himself to be both "king" and "god." (II Thessalonians 2:4) The Antichrist will be sitting on David's throne when Christ returns the second time.

God did promise that the coming Messiah would re-establish and sit upon David's throne in the Millennial Age. (Isaiah 9:7, Luke 1:32-33) Figuratively speaking, Jesse's tree has been cut down; only the rotting stump remains. But as new growth can come from a dead stump, so also can God restore life to the dead. The new, restored life coming from the stump of Jesse and given the name of Branch, has previously been identified as Yeshua—Jesus.

The Spirit of Yahweh (LORD) will rest on Yeshua the Branch in His earthly form. *"For God was pleased to have **all** His fullness dwell in Him."* (Colossians 1:19) *"The Spirit of wisdom, understanding, counsel, power, and knowledge will rest on Him, as well as the fear of the LORD."* (Isaiah 11:2) The spiritual gifts listed here are only a sampling of the spiritual gifts that are listed in the New Testament. Jesus had them all and infinitely more. He was Immanuel, as *"God became flesh and dwelt among us for awhile."* (John 1)

The last thing listed in Isaiah 11:2 is "the fear of the LORD." Here, the Hebrew word *yirah* is translated into English as "fear." This Hebrew word can also mean "reverence." It would seem that reverence would come closer to the emotion felt by Jesus toward His Father.

John 5:27 says: *"And He* (God) *has given Him* (Jesus) *authority to judge because He is the Son of Man."* God the Father has only given this authority to His Son and to no one else, ever. His judgments are righteous judgments, straight from His Father. In Isaiah 11:3 the Branch is given the right to make righteous judgment. *"He will not judge by what He sees with His eyes, or decide by what He hears with His ears; but with righteousness He will judge the needy, with justice He will give decisions for the poor of the earth."* As humans, we judge by what we see and hear. Sometimes we only see and hear partially, jump to conclusions, and

Jesus, the Branch

make wrong judgments. Jesus is not subject to these human frailties. He is literally above it all. He looks upon and judges our hearts. I Samuel 16:7 tells us: *"...Man looks at the outward appearance, but the LORD looks at the heart."* Since Jesus is the only one who has received authority to make righteous judgments, and the Branch of Isaiah Chapter 11 has the same authority, then again, the Branch must be Jesus and the whole of Chapter 11 is talking about Him.

"Branch" then becomes a code word for Jesus, as do all the other names and titles attributed to Him thus far. Look for them as you study Isaiah.

The Coming Peace

Isaiah Chapter 65, as well as Revelation Chapter 21, both echo what Isaiah says in Chapter 11:6-9: *"The wolf will live with the lamb, the leopard will lie down with the goat, the calf and the lion, and the yearling together; and a little child will lead them. The cow will feed with the bear, their young will lie down together, and the lion will eat straw like the ox. The infant will play near the hole of the cobra, and the young child will put his hand into the viper's nest. They will neither harm nor destroy on all My holy mountain, for the earth will be full of the knowledge of the LORD as the waters cover the sea."*

As mentioned earlier in this study, "in that day" and other similar phrases almost always refer to the end times. You will get confirmation of this by the content of the context. In large part, Isaiah Chapter 11 has been talking about conditions at the end of the Tribulation period and the beginning of the 1,000 year Millennial reign of Christ. Verses 10 and 11 continue to speak about the revived **Root of Jesse** (another code word for Jesus), that "in that day" the nations would rally to Him. This will occur after the Tribulation period. *"In that day, the **Lord** (who?) will reach out His hand a second time to reclaim the remnant that is left of His people...."*

If the Lord Jesus is going to reach out His hand a second time to His people, that begs the question: When did He reach out His hand the first time? This may seem like a rhetorical question to us, but neither hand extension had occurred when Isaiah wrote this. Isaiah writes quite extensively in Chapter 53 (and other places, which we will study later) about some of the conditions surrounding the Messiah at His first physical coming. As Jesus later confirmed in Luke Chapter 19, the Jewish people did not recognize the first hand extension. Jesus wept over His people because He knew about the tragic persecution they were going to go through, because they did not recognize the time of God's coming to them.

Then, as now, the majority of the Jewish people were only looking for one coming of the Messiah. They were looking for the Lion of the Tribe of Judah (Revelation 5:5); the One Who would throw off the yoke of the Roman Empire. They were not looking for the Suffering Servant. However, Old Testament prophets taught, and Jesus confirmed, He would come again a second time as King of Kings and Lord of Lords.

Even after 2,000 years the vast majority of the Jewish people still have not recognized the first coming of their Messiah. But make no mistake, the remnant of the Jewish people will recognize the One they have pierced, at the end of the Tribulation period. The second time He visibly returns, the Jews will recognize His extended nail-pierced hand. **The Root of Jesse, the Branch, will accomplish this.**

Salvation

Chapter 12 also begins with "in that day" and continues the main theme of Chapter 11. It is the newly re-established personal relationship with His people Israel that will take place in the future.

In the first three verses of Chapter 12, you'll find the word "salvation" used three times. "Salvation" is the English word translated directly from the Hebrew root word *yasa*. *Yeshua* is the Aramaic form of this Hebrew root word. As you might recall, *Yeshua* was the name the angel told Joseph to call the Child that Mary was to give birth to. *Yeshua* means "YAHWEH saves," "salvation," "to save, deliver," etc. Jesus was to do all of these things, and more, in fulfillment of His Name. Here in this chapter is the first time that Isaiah uses the word "salvation." As we continue to study Isaiah, when you see the word salvation, in your mind substitute the Hebrew word *Yeshua*. *Yeshua*, in its Hebrew form, can be a verb, a noun, or a proper noun. When you substitute the English "salvation" for the Hebrew "Yeshua," see if Yeshua will fit as a proper noun. Be careful in doing this. Most scholars will not agree with being this liberal with the text. It is offered as an exercise in exploring latent or subliminal possibilities in the texts concerning Jesus.

Part of the purpose of this study is to show the many ways in which Isaiah saw Jesus' glory. God revealed to Isaiah, 250 years in advance, the name of Cyrus, king of the Medes and Persians, who would free the Jewish people from Babylonian bondage. Since God showed Isaiah so much about Jesus (of which we yet have much to study), it would not be unusual for God to also reveal His Son's Name. God showed His propensity to do so by naming Cyrus. Maybe we have just overlooked that possibility because Jesus' Hebrew name is used many times in Isaiah's writings, most usually translated as a verb or noun, but not a proper noun. Below is one such possibility. Other possibilities will be explored as we come to the text.

Let's use Isaiah 12:3 as an insight into the possibilities. *"With joy you will draw water from the wells of* **salvation** (wells of Yeshua, wells of Jesus)." To start with, drawing water from the wells reminds us of Jesus' encounter with the Samaritan woman. We can find this account in Luke Chapter 4. Jesus asked the Samaritan woman at the well for a drink. After she essentially said "no," Jesus answered her, telling her that if she knew the gift of God, Who it was that was speaking to her, and asked, He would have given her "Living Water." Jesus told her that everyone who drinks from the water of this well will be thirsty again, but whoever drinks water from His well will never thirst again. *"Indeed, the Water I give will become a spring of Water welling up to eternal life."* This would be water from Yeshua's well…the wells of salvation. We have come full circle back to Isaiah 12:3. Another example comes from John 7:37-39: *"On the last and greatest day of the feast, Jesus stood and said in a loud voice, 'If a man is thirsty, let him come to Me and drink. Whoever believes in Me, as the Scripture has said, streams of Living Water will flow from within him.' By this He meant the Spirit, whom those who believe in Him were later to receive."*

Revelation Chapter 22 tells us that this Water of Life, this Living Water, a code word for the Holy Spirit, would be a free gift from God. This living water is a free gift from Jesus and is given to anybody who believes in Him. This free gift, coming from the wells of Yeshua, was prophesied by Isaiah when he told us *"With joy you will draw Water from the wells of (Jesus)…,"* both now and in the future; both Jew and Gentile.

Have you been thirsty all your life but never able to satisfy your thirst? Jesus offers you the free gift of Living Water. He wants you to come to Him. Just believe in Him, trust Him…and drink.

The Future Wrath of God

Chapter 13 starts out as an oracle, or prophecy, against Babylon. Like so many times in the writings of the prophets, it starts out on one subject, but midway through interjects prophecies unrelated to the beginning topic. We have such a case here in Chapter 13. Beginning at verse 9 and continuing through verse 13, we have end-time prophecy.

Verse 9 says: *"See, the day of the* LORD *is coming—a cruel day, with* **wrath** *and fierce anger to make the land desolate and destroy the sinners within it."* There is only one "day of the LORD," the day of the Lord's wrath, and that is at the end of the Tribulation period, when the Lord—Yeshua, Jesus—returns to fight against the nations. Revelation Chapter 6 tells us when the day of the Lord's wrath begins. It begins during the Tribulation period. Revelation 6:16-17 says: *"They called to the mountains and the rocks, 'Fall on us and hide us from the face of Him who sits on the throne and from the wrath of the Lamb! For the great day of Their* **wrath** *has come, and who can stand?'"* Here we have strong evidence that Isaiah and the Apostle John are talking about the same event. The evidence gets even stronger in Isaiah 13:10, because Jesus used the same description in Matthew Chapter 24 when describing some of the events and conditions on the earth at the time of His Second Coming: *"The stars of heaven and their constellations will not show their light. The rising sun will be darkened and the moon will not give its light."*

Several references to the Second Coming and some of the earthly conditions that would manifest themselves leading up to the Tribulation period have been presented. A more detailed look of conditions that will present themselves in ever-increasing frequency leading up to and during the Tribulation period is in order. Plagues, earthquakes, out-of-control weather, famine, people going back and forth to seek knowledge, a falling away or a rebellion against the true faith, the nations hating Israel and Christians as well, will now be briefly looked at.

Jesus, the Branch

Concerning plagues, the AIDS virus is killing almost two million people per year worldwide. There is a new strain of the AIDS virus, resistant to all forms of medical treatment, coming to the fore. There was the SARS virus outbreak of 2003, which killed about 15 percent of those affected. There was great concern at the time that it would become an epidemic. Now there is great concern that a virus called the bird flu, which has a 70 percent kill rate in humans, will become an epidemic; not to mention the Ebola virus, tuberculosis, malaria, and so many others, that are becoming resistant to antibiotics. Add to this the biological weapons that many nations possess, and we have a scenario that parallels the descriptions of famine and plague found in Revelation 6:8, 11:6, and 16:21 ... if these weapons and viruses are released.

In the 1940s, the decade that Israel was reborn, there were 51 earthquakes worldwide that were 6.0 or higher on the Richter scale. In the 1950s, there were 475; in the 1980s, there were 1,085; and the 1990s, 1,514 earthquakes worldwide. In Matthew 24:7-8 we read *"Nation will rise against nation, and kingdom against kingdom. There will be famines and earthquakes in various places. All these are the beginnings of birth pangs."*

Concerning our weather, we had 1,717 tornadoes in the United States in 2004. That was 300 more than the previous record, set in 1998. The year 2004 was the most expensive year in history from damage caused by hurricanes. But 2004 pales in comparison to the damage and death caused by hurricanes in 2005. The year 2005 turned out to have more damage and death from hurricanes and other related natural phenomena than the previous ten years combined. There have been catastrophic floods all over the United States in the last ten years. Many places in the United States have set record snowfall levels, either in single snow events or in monthly or seasonal snow totals. These weather extremes are occurring all over the world (i.e., the East Asian tsunami of December, 2004, the huge Pakistani earthquake of 2005, etc.).

What is going on in the field of genetics is both astounding and appalling. The amount of knowledge and progress that has been gained through research into genetic engineering is astounding. Many advances have been made benefiting human health and the quality of life. But it is appalling that genetically-engineered mice have human ears growing out of their backs for transplantation to humans with ear injuries or defects. Human genes and DNA are being fused into many different kinds of animals to grow human brains, blood, and other spare parts transplantable to humans. There is even talk of a "humanzee," a human chimpanzee chimera with certain human abilities, going around in some philosophical and bioethical circles. Science is at the crossroads of being able to create new species at will. The human species is trying to gain the creative knowledge of God.

The Prophet Daniel, in Chapter 12:4, says that *"Many will go here and there to increase knowledge."* The ability to go here and there, to and fro, back and forth, has been made practical since the 1940s through modern transportation systems and communication systems. We can go here and there, back and forth, around the world in a matter of seconds with our computers, in order to increase knowledge. The Hebrew word *"yada"* that is translated as "knowledge" can also mean insight or wisdom, as well as the "creative knowledge of God." Daniel foresaw a time that he labeled "the end times" in which men would be actively seeking the creative knowledge of God, such as people are doing today.

The Apostle Paul taught the Thessalonians that right before the Tribulation period begins, there would be a "falling away" within the Church; a rebellion against the true teaching of Scripture. What would be taught as scriptural truth would in fact be a departure from what is considered orthodox teaching, and a departure from the faith. Jesus told us in Matthew 24:9 that Christians would be hated of all nations. Zechariah 14:2 implies that Israel would be hated of all nations, since all nations are going to come against her in battle to destroy her.

Some people would say that we have had most of these aforementioned calamities throughout history, and that is true. Jesus taught us that when we see all of these signs concentrated into one small time frame, all occurring simultaneously in ever-increasing intensity, we are to look up, because our Salvation draws near. We are living in a time of an unprecedented number of the signs and events that Jesus said would occur in the last generation (Matthew 24:31).

The above list is not inclusive of all the signs given in Scripture to indicate the end times, but it is representative.

As much as possible in your study and presentation of the gospel, remember to let Scripture prove Scripture. Let Scripture explain

Scripture, let Scripture give insight to other Scriptures. Be sure you do not take verses out of context and try to make them say something they were never intended to say.

Tribulation Survivors More Scarce Than Pure Gold

Zechariah 14:16 tells us that there will be survivors from all the nations that have attacked Jerusalem during the Tribulation, but in Isaiah 13:12, God says He will make man more scarce than pure gold. This will be the result of the mass deaths that will take place, as described in Revelation concerning Armageddon and God's judgments against mankind. Isaiah 13:14 then goes back to his prophecy against Babylon. Keep in mind when Isaiah wrote this, the Assyrian empire was just coming into power. It would be another 150 years before the Babylonian empire (which is present-day Iraq) came into its own. The Babylonians would take Judah and Jerusalem captive and destroy the temple in 587 B.C. In verse 17 Isaiah says that God will raise up the Medes, which includes the Persians (present-day Iran), to exercise His judgment against the Babylonians for what they did to Israel. Isaiah further indicates that once the city of Babylon is destroyed, *"she will never be inhabited or lived in through all generations...."*

Babylon was quite a city in its heyday. It had walls surrounding the city. According to fifth century B.C. documents, this wall was a little over ten miles long on each side, over 300 feet high, and 86 feet wide. On top of its ramparts there was room enough for a four-horse chariot to pass. Saddam Hussein, when he was in power, did major excavations at the site. He offered a one-million dollar reward to any engineer who could figure out how to duplicate what the ancients did regarding the Hanging Gardens of Babylon. He wanted to restore the city to its former glory. Sculptures of himself and Nebuchad-nezzar, for self-glorification, were in the plans. Saddam Hussein is no longer in power. His plans were thwarted because God said Babylon will never again be inhabited throughout all generations.

The Babylon of Revelation Chapter 17, which sits on seven hills and rules over the kings of the earth, could possibly be the city of Rome and the revised Roman Empire hinted at in the book of Daniel. At any rate, it will be a mirror image of false religion, economic power and military might that the original Babylon represented. Like the original Babylon, it will come to destroy Israel, but this time God will intervene and the outcome will be different.

Faith Questions

1. What kind of fruit will the Branch bear?
2. What will living conditions be like when the Prince of Peace comes?
3. What will living conditions be like during the Tribulation? (Matthew 24)
4. When do the two "hand extensions" of Jesus occur?

Lesson 11

ISAIAH CHAPTERS 14 THROUGH 16
SATAN'S AMBITION

Isaiah 14:3 continues the prophecy against Babylon. More specifically, it is against the king of Babylon. Beginning at verse 12, through verse 15, the subject person changes. The king of Babylon has never fallen from heaven, but there is one who did: Satan. Here we have some insight into Satan and what motivates him. Satan said in his heart, *"I will ascend to heaven; I will raise my throne above the stars of God; I will sit enthroned on the mount of assembly, on the utmost heights of the sacred mountain, I will ascend above the tops of the clouds; I will make myself like the Most High. But you are brought down to the grave, to the depths of the pit."* This is not only a description of Satan and his attitude but a prophecy concerning his final disposition.

Pride was Satan's greatest motivator. His self-image was so puffed up that he not only wanted to make himself equal to God, he wanted to set his throne higher than God's throne, making himself greater and more powerful than God. Let's turn to Ezekiel Chapter 28. As Isaiah started out with a lament against the king of Babylon, so Ezekiel starts out with a lament against the king of Tyre. However, it soon becomes apparent that Ezekiel could not possibly be speaking about the king of Tyre. The king of Babylon and the king of Tyre, as Ezekiel and Isaiah described them, have attributes similar to Satan's and would come to a similar demise at the end of their lives. Satan was the real power behind the king of Babylon and the king of Tyre.

We will take this commentary of Ezekiel's verse by verse, starting at 28:12b: *"You were the model of perfection, full of wisdom and perfect in beauty. You were in Eden, the garden of God..."* There were four individuals present in the garden of God as recorded in Genesis 3. They were God, Adam and Eve, and Satan, the serpent. The king of Tyre was not present, so this part of Scripture cannot be speaking of the king of Tyre. Therefore, which one of the four mentioned above are these passages talking about? Let's read on.

"...every precious stone adorned you: ruby, topaz and emerald, chrysolite, onyx and jasper, sapphire, turquoise and beryl." This eliminates Adam and Eve because the most they had on were leaves. *"Your settings and mountings were made of gold; on the day you were **created** they were prepared."* Well, that eliminates God. He is from everlasting to everlasting. It should be noted here that Satan is a created being, as opposed to Jesus being the only begotten Son. Begotten, not created.

Satan had nine precious stones adorning him. The high priest of God serving in the temple wore an *ephod*, or vest, with 12 precious stones on it. The number 12 represents God's completion, or completeness, and also represented the 12 tribes of Israel. According to the book of Hebrews, Jesus is our High Priest. Although Satan was the model of perfection, full of wisdom and perfect in beauty, he was still a created being and his having nine precious stones instead of 12 reflects that. He could never completely fulfill the duties of the high priest nor was he created to do so. Jesus alone represents God's completion and fulfills the role of High Priest.

Continuing in verse 14: *"You were anointed as a guardian cherub, for so I ordained you. You were on the holy mount of God; you walked among the fiery stones. You were blameless in your ways from the day you were created till wickedness was found in you."* Satan was created an angel, as were all the angels. He had the high rank of guardian cherub. The pride he had in himself because of his beauty and wisdom and high rank started to go to his head. He began to think more highly of himself than was warranted. The Scripture tells us that "pride goes before a fall" (Proverbs 16:18).

The rest of the Scriptures quoted below show Satan's fall from heaven to his complete destruction in the lake of fire at the end of the age.

Going on with verses 16-19, we read: *"Through your widespread trade you were filled with violence, and you sinned. So I drove you in disgrace from the mount of God, and I expelled you, O guardian cherub, from among the fiery stones. Your heart became* **proud** *on account of your beauty, and you corrupted your wisdom because of your splendor. So I threw you to the earth; I made a spectacle of you before kings. By your many sins and dishonest trade you have desecrated your sanctuaries. So I made fire come out from you, and it consumed you, and I reduced you to ashes on the ground in the sight of all who were watching. All the nations who knew you are appalled that you have come to a horrible end and will be no more."* This is a prophetic promise and an encapsulated picture of Satan from beginning to end. Satan can depend on it.

Pride Goes Before a Fall

Pride is what started the ball rolling in Satan's downfall. All of the emotions that Satan felt, like violence, corrupted wisdom, greed (looking at what he didn't have instead of looking at what he had), anger and rage all had their roots in pride. Pride is what Satan will use against us. It is his best tool to use against Christians and non-believers alike. Pride is the root of theft. I do not "have" but I deserve to "have." Pride is the root of addictions. "My friends got addicted to this drug, but I'm stronger than they are. It won't happen to me!" Pride is the root of our comparisons. "I'm taller than you are, I'm prettier than you are, I'm richer than you are, I'm more educated than you, my job position is higher than yours, I'm not fat like you. Therefore, I am better than you." Pride is what puffs up our self-image beyond what it should be. Pride is responsible for more wars, more quarrels, more hurt feelings, more divorces, more split churches. Pride is the root of hatred, anger, jealousies, greed, violence, and racial tensions. Again, pride is the best tool Satan has in his arsenal to use against Christians and non-believers alike.

Pride is the source of rebellion—"I'd rather do it my way." Pride was Satan's source of rebellion against God. It is the source of our rebellion against God. It is and will be the source of the rebellion and falling away within the Church, as mentioned in II Thessalonians 2:3. Pride is the source of the lawless one (Satan incarnate). It is our source of lawlessness, to either be above the law or have disregard for the law. The laws of God, as well as the laws of man, were intended for someone else, not us. In Deuteronomy Chapter 8, the Jewish people were warned when they were about to enter the promised land, that when they became prosperous not to become so proud as to think all of their wealth was the result of the power and strength of their hands. God said not to have false pride. It would be God that would give them the ability to produce wealth.

Satan pulled out his best tool (weapon) to use against his strongest, most formidable opponent, Jesus. In Matthew Chapter 4, after Jesus spent 40 days in the wilderness fasting, Satan said to Him: *"If you are the Son of God tell the stones to become bread."* (Verse 3) And in verse 6, *"Then the devil took Him to…the highest point of the temple. 'If you are the Son of God,' he said, 'throw yourself down…'"* Each time, Satan appealed to whatever pride he tried to evoke from Jesus concerning His title and position as Son of God. Jesus would have none of it. Jesus proves His superior willpower, His superior knowledge, and His superior love over, above and beyond what Satan lost when he fell.

When Jesus was hanging on the cross, the passersby shouted the same insults to Jesus, using the same phraseology as Satan used. *"Save yourself! Come down from the cross, **if you are the Son of God**."* (Matthew 27:39 and 40) Considering the physical, mental and spiritual agony Jesus was in, way beyond what we can even imagine, the temptation to come down off the cross would have been great. Jesus had answered this question about saving his physical life in Matthew 26:53 and 54: *"Do you think I cannot call on My Father, and He will at once put at My disposal more than twelve legions of angels? But how then would the Scriptures be fulfilled that say it must happen in this way?"*

Jesus knew He could have stopped His suffering at the garden of Gethsemane, He could have stopped it during the beatings and the floggings, and He could have stopped it while He was suffering intensely on the cross by calling in twelve legions of angels. But He didn't.

What about the angels in heaven? Were they begging and pleading with the Father to release them and their awesome power to stop these terrible scenes? If the Father had released them, how then would the Scriptures be fulfilled that say it must happen this way?

Jesus stayed on the cross. He stayed there until it was finished; demonstrating His perfect personification of love for us. Jesus stayed loving and humble. He did not consider equality with God as a thing to be grasped. (Philippians Chapter 2) Jesus would not, and did not, fall prey to pride as Satan did. Jesus didn't sin and He didn't fall. Satan offered all the kingdoms of the world to Jesus, trying to stir up pride through greed. Jesus quoted Scripture to Satan, and Satan left.

Sometimes, people have pride in their particular denomination. We need to be careful about that, because it may result in looking down on other denominations for the wrong reasons. When you are looking down, you are not looking up. We could say instead, "I am pleased to be a Lutheran, or Methodist, or Baptist or…."

In the Church, Satan will use all of the above tactics. He is not a funny looking man in a red suit, with horns and a pitchfork. Satan was beautiful in heaven, and he can be beautiful within the Church. It was mentioned earlier in this study that Satan wanted to destroy and damage the things of God. It is understood—it is a given—that Satan wants to scatter the flock, and get people to turn away from God. So if one wants to scatter the flock and get people to turn away from God, where would you start? The seminary? The head of the church body? The pastorate? The church treasurer? Strategically-placed parishioners? Yes, all of these and more.

In II Corinthians 11:13-16 we read: *"For such men are false apostles, deceitful workmen, masquerading as apostles of Christ. And no wonder, for Satan himself masquerades as an angel of light. It is not surprising, then, if his servants masquerade as servants of righteousness. Their end will be what their actions deserve."* Within the Church, from top to bottom, Satan's servants can masquerade as "servants of righteousness." Matthew Chapter 7 says we will "know them by their fruits."

We must put on the whole armor of God, as outlined in Ephesians Chapter 6, and have an accurate knowledge of Scripture. This will help us stand and oppose those powerful forces that masquerade as servants of righteousness. As mentioned earlier in this study, people without knowledge and understanding will come to ruin. They will be exiled, taken captive by Satan, and they will not even know it until it is too late.

The Apostle Paul speaks a couple of times of having pride in a positive and loving way (i.e., II Corinthians 7:9), but more often he warns his churches about the need to have humility, the opposite of pride (i.e., Titus 3:2).

Faith Questions

1. There are seven verses in Proverbs concerning pride. What do they teach us? (A concordance is needed.)
2. Based on the Scripture in this lesson, what strikes you most about Satan?
3. How can you guard against false pride?
4. What are some effective ways in which you can help prideful people?

Lesson 12

ISAIAH CHAPTERS 17 AND 18
THE LORD COMES FOR HIS BRIDE

Isaiah Chapter 17 starts out with a prophecy concerning Damascus. *"See, Damascus will no longer be a city but will become a heap of ruins."* Damascus, Syria is still a viable city today. This prophecy has not yet been fulfilled. With all the tensions that are going on in the Middle East, it could be fulfilled at any time. It may even be that Damascus will be a victim of the Tribulation. One thing is for certain: *"**In that day** men will look to their **Maker** and turn their eyes to the **Holy One of Israel**."* (verse 7) *"**In that day** their strong cities…will all be desolation* (because) *you have forgotten God your Savior; you have not remembered the **Rock**, your Fortress."* (Verses 9 and 10) It sounds as though there will be cities and nations throughout the earth that were once considered Christian, who knew God the Savior, the Rock, Jesus, but somehow lost faith in Him, got off the narrow path, and took the broad road, the one that leads to destruction. It has been said that the true Christian faith is only one generation away from dying out, if we do not pass it on to the next generation. Of course, God will not permit that to happen.

Isaiah Chapter 18 starts out as a prophecy against Cush. In verse 3 Isaiah begins his prophetic promises concerning another future time. He is addressing not just a specific country or location; he is addressing all the people who live on the earth. He says: *"…when a Banner is raised on the mountains, you will see it."* Does the word "banner" strike a note with you? We sort of passed over it in Isaiah 11:10. It said *"…the Root of Jesse* (which is a code word for Jesus) *will stand as a Banner for the peoples."* Jesus will stand as a Banner—something that everybody can see. Isaiah is addressing all the people of the earth. Jesus told us in Matthew 24 that *"…the sign of the Son of Man will appear in the sky and **all** the nations of the earth will mourn."* (verse 30a) A banner can be like a sign, and Jesus will be the Sign.

When the Trumpet Sounds

There is another element in Isaiah 18:3 that should be examined. Isaiah says that just as a banner is raised for all to see, so also, *"When a trumpet sounds, you will hear it."* Again, Isaiah is addressing all the people that live on earth. The only time that God speaks to all the nations of the earth is during the end times. Isaiah is saying to the people of the end times, *"When a trumpet sounds, you will hear it."* Let's look at what the New Testament writers associate with the sounding of the Hebrew *shofar* (ram's horn, trumpet).

The Apostle Paul tells us in I Corinthians 15:52: *"…in a flash, in the twinkling of an eye, at the last **trumpet**. For the **trumpet** will sound, the dead will be raised imperishable, and we will be changed."* Here, Paul is associating the trumpet sound with the Rapture. Again, he instructs the Thessalonians in 4:16: *"For the Lord Himself will come down from heaven, with a loud command, with the voice of the archangel and with the **trumpet** call of God, and the dead in Christ will rise first. After that, we who are still alive and are left will be <u>caught up</u> with them in the clouds to meet the Lord in the air."* The trumpet is ushering in the Rapture! Jesus tells us in Matthew 24:31, speaking for Himself, *"He will send His angels with a loud **trumpet** call, and they will gather His elect from the four winds, from one end of the heavens to the other."* There can be no doubt that when the heavenly trumpet sounds for the first time during the end times, that the Rapture will occur immediately following.

The Lord Comes for His Bride

The word "rapture," as used here, does not occur in the Bible. Yet it is frequently used to describe a future event concerning the Church—those who confess Jesus. An explanation seems to be in order. The Apostle Paul uses the Greek word *harpazo*, which is translated as "caught up." This still does not give us the word "rapture." The Latin word used to translate the Greek word "harpazo" into the Latin Vulgate Bible was "*raptus.*" From the Latin "raptus" we get the English word "rapture." The word "rapture" in English can imply being <u>carried off</u> in a spiritual sense. The Believing Church uses the word "rapture" to encapsulate the thought of being "caught up" to Jesus when He comes for His Church. The word "rapture" then becomes a way to capture the picture of, or explain the multiplicity of, events surrounding the mass resurrections and translations into heaven. Paul describes these events in I Thessalonians Chapter 4, and the Prophet Daniel also describes them in Daniel 12:2-3: *"Multitudes who sleep in the dust of the earth will awaken: some to everlasting life, others to shame and everlasting contempt. Those who are wise will shine like the brightness of the heavens, and those who lead many to righteousness, like the stars for ever and ever."*

There are several theories in circulation concerning when this Rapture will occur. Some even go so far as to set dates. Jesus told His disciples in Acts Chapter 1, concerning their question of "When?," that it was not for them to know the times or the dates, and this applies to us today, as well. The question within the Church has always been, "When does the Rapture occur in relation to the Tribulation and Millennial reign of Christ?" Most believe that it will occur at the beginning of the Tribulation period. Those who ascribe to this timeline give very convincing proofs from Scripture as their reasons for adhering to this theory. Likewise, some believe this will occur at the midway point of the seven-year Tribulation period. Some in the Church believe it will occur at the end of the Tribulation period, and some don't believe it will happen at all! All seem to vigorously defend their positions, while at the same time, trying to tear down the case made by others who hold other positions, and giving reasons why those views could not possibly be correct.

The Jewish Holy Days: Another Possibility for End Times Fulfillment

Well, there is nothing like throwing a fly into the ointment, putting a monkey wrench into the gears, and other appropriate clichés. So let's take the time to develop another theory for you to consider.

There are seven sacred assemblies the Jewish people are to observe at their appointed times each year, as God commanded the Israelites. These are: Passover (Hebrew *Pesach*), Unleavened Bread *(Hag Ha'Matzah)*, First Fruits *(Sfirat Ha'Omer)*, the Feast of Weeks *(Shavuot)*, the Feast of Trumpets *(Yom T'Ruah)*, the Day of Atonement *(Yom Kippur)*, and the Feast of Tabernacles *(Sukkot)*. These are found in Leviticus Chapter 23. We will not go into any great detail about these sacred assemblies beyond what is needed to provide evidence of their correlation with Christian holidays and observances. You, the reader, are encouraged to research these sacred assemblies on your own to learn more.

Passover is the Jewish tradition of observing what God did for the Israelites while in captivity in Egypt. They were to sacrifice a lamb, without spot or blemish, and smear its sacrificial blood on the door posts so that God would not pass judgment on their first-born sons. They were covered by the blood from the wrath of God. So part of the Jewish tradition on this day, in observance of how God protected them while in Egypt, was for the priests to take an unblemished lamb, and sacrifice it upon the altar of God at 3 o'clock in the afternoon on Passover. Early in the morning of Passover the lambs that had been presented for sacrifice were inspected by the priests to make sure they were unblemished. Not one of their bones could be broken. This inspection was to be completed by nine o'clock in the morning.

Jesus also was inspected by the chief priests very early, in the wee hours of Passover morning. They could find no blemish, so they trumped one up. Jesus hung on the cross from 9 o'clock in the morning until He expired at 3 o'clock in the afternoon. At the exact time the priests were sacrificing the unblemished, sacrificial lamb in the temple and sprinkling its blood on the altar of God, our real, unblemished Sacrificial Lamb, who was bleeding and in agony on the cross, said *"It is finished."* The real, unblemished Sacrificial Lamb had no broken bones, either. (John 19:33, Psalm 34:20) He came not to abolish the law, but to fulfill it.

The Lord Comes for His Bride

Some of you may have participated in a Seder meal ("*seder*" means "order"), a symbolic Jewish meal that occurs on the first evening of Passover. You would remember that part where the unleavened bread was hidden away in a cloth, out of sight. As this piece of unleavened bread was hidden away out of sight, so the body of our Lord Jesus, after His crucifixion, was hidden away out of sight in the tomb. Later in the Seder order, the hidden piece of bread is brought forth with blessing, representing Christ's resurrection.

Unbeknownst to the Jews, three of their sacred assemblies (Passover, Unleavened Bread and First Fruits), were a foreshadow of things to come concerning the death, burial, and resurrection of Jesus Christ. The vast majority of Jewish people don't understand this even now, but they will.

Jesus died on Passover and was in the tomb on the Feast of Unleavened Bread. The day after Unleavened Bread was First Fruits, the day Jesus rose from the dead. First Fruits was an agricultural holiday. The very first sheaf of grain was to be presented to God, in acknowledgment of His blessing. This was in advance of the major harvest that was to come.

Jesus arose from the dead on First Fruits, representing the first of the resurrection harvest that God would provide. The Apostle Paul called Christ the "First Fruits," and all his Jewish listeners knew exactly what he meant. Fifty days after First Fruits came the Feast of Weeks. This is where the beginning of the whole new grain harvest was presented to God.

On the Church's day of Pentecost, we celebrate the giving of the Holy Spirit to Jesus' disciples and the birth of the Church as we know it. This birth of the Church, this giving of the Holy Spirit, occurs fifty days after the resurrection. "*Pente*" in Greek means fifty. It is no accident that the beginning harvest of souls falls exactly on the Jewish Feast of Weeks. Take a moment to ponder the implication of this.

We have Jesus being crucified on Passover, in the tomb on the Feast of Unleavened Bread, being raised on First Fruits, and the giving of the Holy Spirit on the Feast of Weeks. So what is next in the Christian calendar of events? What is the next thing to happen to the Church? Could it possibly be the Rapture? And if so, would it follow the previous precedent of having major Christian events occurring on the major Jewish sacred assembly days? What is the next sacred Jewish assembly day? Is it not the Feast of Trumpets? For the Church, what is going to happen at "the sound of the trumpet?" Is it reasonable to think that these events, too, may also coincide with each other?

There are two Jewish sacred assemblies left after the Feast of Trumpets: the Day of Atonement, and the Feast of Tabernacles. There are two major Christian events left after the Rapture: the Second Coming of Jesus, and a new heaven and a new earth. If the Rapture would occur on the Feast of Trumpets (and many Jewish Messianic Believers think this will be the case), and Jesus' Second Coming occurs on the Day of Atonement, then can we speculate also from these two sacred assemblies the amount of time that might occur between the Rapture and the Second Coming?

There are ten days between the Jewish Feast of Trumpets and the Day of Atonement. If we use Daniel's reckoning time of one day equaling one year, then there could be as many as ten years between the Rapture and the Second Coming. This would place the Rapture up to three years before the beginning of the Tribulation period.

The Bride of Christ

Jesus often referred to the Church as His Bride. Jesus told His disciples in John 14 that in His Father's house were many rooms; that He was going there to prepare a place for them, and if He was going to prepare a place for them, He would come back and take them with Him, back to His Father's house. The image here was very clear to His Jewish listeners. It was precisely the same ceremony used for a Jewish wedding.

In the Jewish tradition, when a young man saw a young woman whom he thought would make a good wife, he and his father would go to the prospective bride's father to draw up a contract of marriage. When the terms of the contract were agreed upon, the young man would offer the young woman a cup of wine. The young woman could then either accept the cup, or reject it. If she accepted the cup, she would in effect be saying "yes" to the proposal. In saying yes, she was agreeing

The Lord Comes for His Bride

to place herself under the provision, protection, love and authority of the young man.

The young man would then go back to his father's house and start building a room addition on to it. This would be a place for him and his new bride to live. No one knew how long it would take for the young man to build this room addition; it may take months. When the roof was finally on, and all that was left were some final touches, everyone knew—including the bride—the time was getting close for the groom to return for her. No one knew for sure exactly when the groom would finish his building project, but all signs indicated that it was close.

The watchword for the bride and wedding party was to "be ready," for no one knew the day or the hour when the groom would return. When the groom did finally arrive, he quickly whisked his bride back to his father's house to begin the celebration. The Jewish custom at the time of Christ was for the wedding celebration to last seven to ten days after the groom came for the bride.

When Jesus comes for His Bride, to take her back to His Father's house, there will be a huge celebration in heaven. Will it last for up to ten years, at which time the Church (the Bride) will mount white horses and return with Christ at His Second Coming? (Revelation 17:14, 19:11-14) It just might be. The length of time that the Bride will be in heaven waiting to return with Jesus can be questioned, but not the event. This theory is only speculation, as are all the other theories. One of these theories will probably prove to be correct. It might prove to be a good idea to keep your spiritual eyes open around the Jewish New Year *(Rosh Ha'Shanah)*, which begins with the Feast of Trumpets *(Yom T'Ruah)*, and the Day of Atonement *(Yom Kippur)*. These days always fall sometime in our months of September or October. You just never know what might happen!

One thing is for sure, at some point—probably in the not-too-distant future—we will be caught up to meet the Lord in the air. Do you have a ticket for this trip? Will you be a passenger? Or will you be left at the boarding gate?

You can't get this ticket online, and you can't get it from your Christian friends. Jesus will give you the ticket He has already paid dearly for. He paid with His life, but He determined that you were worth it.

There is always room for one more on this flight. Will you choose to come on board?

Faith Questions

1. Name the three Jewish Holy Days on which Jesus died, was buried, and then rose from the dead.
2. On which Jewish Holy Day did the Church receive the Holy Spirit?
3. How many days after Passover did the Church receive the Holy Spirit?

Lesson 13

ISAIAH CHAPTERS 19 THROUGH 24
DON'T BE CAUGHT OFF GUARD

Isaiah Chapter 19 gives a prophetic promise about Egypt concerning the "*in that day*" time frame. Before we look closer at this prophecy, let's check out Ezekiel's prophetic promise concerning Egypt in Chapter 29 of his book. Ezekiel tells us about Egypt and its future history as a nation. We will pick up the commentary after Egypt returns from its forty-year captivity in Babylon, starting in verse 13. *"Yet this is what the Sovereign LORD says: 'At the end of forty years I will gather the Egyptians from the nations where they were scattered. I will bring them back from captivity and return them to Upper Egypt, the land of their ancestry. There they will be a lowly kingdom. It will be the lowliest of kingdoms and will never again exalt itself above the other nations. I will make it so weak that it will never again rule over the nations. Egypt will no longer be a source of confidence for the people of Israel but will be a reminder of their sin in turning to her for help. Then they will know that I am the Sovereign LORD.'"*

Ever since this prophecy was made, Egypt has been a lowly kingdom. It has never had the strength or the ability to rule over any other nation or country. Up to the time of this prophecy, Egypt had always been a power to reckon with. In some cases it was the dominant world power. There has been approximately 2,500 years since this prophecy was made for Egypt to prove this prophetic promise wrong. At the time this prophecy was made there was absolutely no reason to believe this would be true. Even Ezekiel, had he been walking by sight, wouldn't have written such a thing. But God says that those who see this truth unfold will not have any excuse: *"Then they will know that I am the Sovereign LORD."*

In Isaiah 19:16-25, the prophet says that the Egyptians and the Assyrians will acknowledge the LORD "in that day." Verses 23-25 read: *"In that day there will be a highway from Egypt to Assyria. The Assyrians will go to Egypt and the Egyptians to Assyria. The Egyptians and the Assyrians will worship together. In that day Israel will be the third, along with Egypt and Assyria, a blessing on the earth. The LORD Almighty will bless them, saying, 'Blessed be Egypt My people, Assyria My handiwork, and Israel My inheritance.'"*

Could it be that Assyria represents the descendants of Ishmael? Could it be that Egypt represents the Gentile nations? If so, then Abraham's family, Ishmael and Isaac, will be reunited again. The Arab and the Jew will worship together, along with the Gentiles. They will all worship the God of Abraham, the God of the Bible. Is Isaiah telling us that there will finally be peace in the family of mankind? Oh, may it be so!

A Terrible Time on Earth

Isaiah Chapter 24 speaks of a very terrible time that is coming upon the earth. (Isaiah 24 and Matthew 24 closely parallel each other.) There is going to be great devastation upon the earth. No one living in that time will be exempt from God's wrath. It will not matter who you are: king, priest, slave, banker, doctor; it just will not matter. Isaiah 24:1 reads: *"See, the LORD is going to lay waste to the earth and devastate it; He will ruin its face and scatter its inhabitants…"* Continuing with verse 5, we read: *"The earth is defiled by its people; they have disobeyed the laws, violated the statutes and broken the everlasting covenant. Therefore a curse consumes the earth; its people must bear their guilt. Therefore earth's inhabitants are burned up and very few are left."*

Picking up with verse 19, Isaiah tells us: *"The earth is broken up, the earth is split asunder, the earth is thoroughly shaken."* The Apostle Peter speaks of similar conditions in II Peter 3:10: *"But the day of the Lord will come like a thief. The heavens will disappear with a roar; the elements will be destroyed by fire, and the earth and everything in it will be laid bare."* As an example of the destruction detailed in the book of Revelation, let's turn to Revelation 16:18-19. *"Then there will come flashes of lightning, rumblings, peals of thunder and a severe earthquake. No earthquake like it has ever occurred since man has been on earth, so tremendous was the quake. The great city split into three parts, and the cities of the nations collapsed. ..."*

Again, Isaiah says that the inhabitants of earth would be very few. Recall his earlier comments about people being more rare than fine gold. Planet earth is not going to be a nice place to be living, considering the things that are prophetically promised to occur during the end times. The issues that God has against mankind are great and too numerous to mention. Many issues have been covered previously in this study, but there is one word given in Isaiah 24:20 that seems to encapsulate everything into one package. That word is "rebellion." Rebellion against God, rebellion against everything God stands for. It is the falling away from God's truth, substituting darkness for light. It is the total spiritual dominance of Satan upon mankind that occurs during the end times.

What Happens to Christians?

So where are the Christians who call Jesus "Lord" in all of this? Are we to go through this Tribulation wrath that is reserved for rebellious, unrepentant people? As stated earlier, there are a few theories concerning this issue. Jesus seems to be giving us some encouragement in this area, beginning in Luke 21:33, when He says *"Heaven and earth will pass away, but My words will never pass away. Be careful, or your heart will be weighed down with dissipation, drunkenness and the anxieties of life, and that day will close on you unexpectedly like a trap. For it will come upon all those who live on the face of the whole earth. Be always on the* **watch***, and* **pray** *that you may be able to* **escape** *all that is about to happen, and that you may be able to stand before the Son of Man."*

God provided Noah and his family the means and the foreknowledge to escape. They did not have to go through the wrath and destruction that God had determined for the earth. They were kept safe on board the ark. When the door of the ark was "sealed," Noah's fate, and the fate of his family, was sealed. By default, the fate of the rest of mankind was also sealed. Noah and his family *"...entered the ark to **escape** the waters of the flood."* (Genesis 7:7) To escape God's judgment and wrath...could it be that Jesus has made provision for His Bride to escape the wrath of God that is to come? The answer is *yes*, and that mechanism for escape is the Rapture. The only other way we as Christians could escape the extreme human suffering that is to come, is to be dead before it happens. In the above verses from Luke, Jesus is not talking to dead people. He is talking to people very much alive and giving them instructions as to how they might escape. Jesus wouldn't do that if there were not a way. The Apostle Paul is very clear in his first letter to the Thessalonians. I Thessalonians 1:10 reads: *"and to wait for His Son from heaven, whom He raised from the dead, Jesus,* **Who rescues us from the coming wrath.***"* Again, in I Thessalonians 5:9, we are told *"For* **God did not appoint us to suffer wrath** *but to receive salvation through our Lord Jesus Christ."* Do not let fear dominate your heart when you read and study the things that are soon coming upon the earth. It is not for you to experience!

Jesus tells us in Luke 21 to *"Be careful, or your heart will be weighed down with dissipation* (self indulgence), *drunkenness and the anxieties of life,"* and, if you're not careful, *"that day will close on you unexpectedly like a trap."* What do you think of when you see the word "trap?" Something we use to snare animals? If that is the case, we would build this trap so that whatever got ensnared in it could not possibly escape. Certainly this is the picture that Jesus is painting. That is why He tells us in Luke 21:36 to *"Be always on the watch...."*

Using Noah and Lot as Examples

Jesus tells us a lot about what **that day** will look like. Some things He told us in a very straightforward way. In other things, He is requiring the listeners/readers to do research. Examples of this are found in Luke Chapter 17, starting with verse 26: *"Just as it was in the days of Noah, so also will it be in the days of the Son of Man. People were eating, drinking, marrying and being given in marriage up to the day Noah entered the ark. Then the flood came and destroyed them all. It was the same as the days of Lot. People were eating and drinking, buying and selling, planting and building. But the day Lot left Sodom, fire and sulfur rained down from* *heaven and destroyed them all. It will be just like this on the day the Son of Man is revealed."*

Jesus said *"just as it was in the days of Noah."* Then He goes on to describe what seems to be fairly normal activity. However, there was actually more to it "in the days of Noah." In order to get a little better picture of what it was like in the days of Noah, let's turn to Genesis Chapter 6, beginning with verse 11. *"Now the earth was corrupt in God's sight and was full of violence. God saw how corrupt the earth had become, for all the people on earth had corrupted their ways. So God said to Noah, 'I am going to put an end to all people, for the earth is filled with violence because of them.'"*

Two of the hallmarks of Noah's day were corruption and violence. We certainly have both in abundance in the world today, and it seems to be getting worse. There is a statistic out there that says in seven states you are more likely to die from a gunshot wound than from an automobile accident. We don't have to tell you about the corruption in the world. It is pandemic. Jesus also said it would be like in the days of Lot. We can find a brief explanation about the days of Lot, recorded in Jude verse 7: *"In a similar way, Sodom and Gomorrah and the surrounding towns gave themselves up to sexual immorality and perversion. They serve as an example of those who suffer the punishment of eternal fire."* Half of our high school students have engaged in sexual activity before they graduate. Sexual infidelity within marriage causes the breakup of thousands of homes, great psychological harm to children, and forces many children into poverty. There is an old saying that goes like this: "As the twig is bent so grows the tree." Many adults never get over what happened to them in childhood. We have widespread addiction to pornography, the scandals of some of the priests, and the AIDS epidemic in Africa, as well as homosexual behavior in this country. It is easy to see the worldwide sexual immorality and perversion that exists. It has been said that if God doesn't soon judge the world, He'll have to dig up Sodom and Gomorrah and apologize to them.

We now have a good idea of what conditions will be like in the days leading up to the Tribulation period and the Second Coming of Jesus Christ. However, Jesus did indicate that in many ways things will be going along fairly normally. People will be getting married, buying and selling, planting and building. For those who aren't watching, it will be unexpected. It will be a total surprise, like walking into a trap from which there is no escape. If you're walking in the woods, and you know that the neighbor boy has set traps there, you will be on the lookout for them so you can avoid stepping on them. If someone else should wander through the same woods not paying any attention to where they are stepping ... well, you get the point. Most people of the earth will not be paying attention and it will come upon them unexpectedly, like a trap.

When it is all over, *"From the ends of the earth we hear singing: 'Glory to the **Righteous One**.'"* Glory to Jesus! (Isaiah 24:16)

Faith Questions

1. How is fulfilled prophecy serving God's purpose?
2. What does God want us to know about Him when we see prophecy fulfilled?
3. Why did God have Noah and his family enter the ark? (Refer to Genesis 7:7)

Lesson 14

ISAIAH CHAPTERS 25 THROUGH 28
AT THE RENEWAL OF ALL THINGS

Isaiah Chapter 25 begins to look forward to the Eden-like conditions that will prevail after the Second Coming. Jesus refers to this time in Matthew 19:28 as *"at the renewal of all things."* Things will be different after this time of renewal. In the aftermath of centuries of lies and deception and war brought on by Satan, Jesus will take the opportunity to set everything straight. One of the things that will happen is described in Isaiah 25:7: *"On this mountain He will destroy the shroud that enfolds all peoples, the sheet that covers all nations."* The message this verse holds for us may not be immediately plain, but when we compare it to other Scriptures, a light can be turned on to help illuminate its meaning.

Let's turn to II Corinthians 3:14-16. Here the Apostle Paul is beginning to speak about the veil Moses would put over his face to keep the Israelites from seeing the fullness of the radiance of God reflected from his face. Speaking of the Jews, Paul begins: *"But their minds were made dull, for to this day the same veil remains whenever the old covenant is read. It has not been removed, because only in **Christ** is it taken away. Even to this day when Moses is read, a veil covers their hearts. But whenever **anyone** turns to the Lord, the veil is taken away."* Paul is telling us that there is a veil, a covering, a shroud, which prevents not only the Jewish people, but Gentiles also, from seeing the truthfulness of God and His Word. When this veil covers the hearts and minds of unbelievers, the gospel becomes foolishness to those who are perishing. There is a key that unlocks this Satanic condition; Paul tells us that *"only in Christ is it taken away."* Whenever **anyone** turns to the Lord, that veil, or covering, that "blindness," is taken away.

To those who would say "Let me get my house in order then I will go to church, or then I'll ask Jesus into my heart;" that is putting the cart before the horse. Not by our actions, not by our works, but only in Jesus Christ is the veil taken away. This veil is the cause of our blindness. We will remain blind to spiritual truth until we ask Jesus to take it away. At the renewal of all things, Jesus will destroy the shroud that enfolds and the sheet that covers, so that spiritual blindness to God's truth will never occur again.

Another thing that will be changed at the renewal of all things is death. Isaiah 25:8 says *"He will swallow up death forever."* It will be no more. It will be a thing of the past. Because of that, God will wipe away the tears from all faces. The death of a loved one, or our own impending death, is perhaps the greatest tragedy and sorrow we have to face. This will all be changed and forever done away with at the renewal of all things, when Jesus Christ comes and reigns in glory upon the earth.

Isaiah 25:9 reads: *"In that day they will say, 'Surely this is our God; we trusted in Him and He saved us. This is the* LORD, *we trusted in Him; let us be glad and rejoice in His* Jesus.*'"* Oops! The Scripture really says **salvation**. We read in Titus 2:11, *"For the grace of God that brings* **salvation** *has appeared to all men."*

We Are to Trust

Isaiah Chapter 26 starts with *"In that day"* which sets the time frame. This is not to say that the entire chapter is dedicated to end-time prophecies. We will highlight some of the attributes of God and His promises to us and to the Jewish people. Isaiah outlines our need to trust the Lord; how He makes our path level, gives grace to the wicked, establishes peace for us, and resurrects us from the dead. That is quite a bit for one chapter to cover, so let's take a closer look.

"Trust in the LORD forever, for the LORD, the LORD is the Rock eternal." (Isaiah 26:4) Trust in the Lord. Sometimes this is a difficult thing to do for believers. Certainly it is easy to trust in the Lord when things are going good. But when times get tough our first inclination many times is to try to figure it out on our own. Trust is tantamount to having faith. So what is faith? Let's turn to the premier faith chapter in the New Testament, Hebrews Chapter 11. This chapter starts out with the definition of what faith is. *"Now faith is being sure of what we hope for and certain of what we do not see. This is what the ancients were commended for."* Therefore, being "sure and certain" becomes the scale by which we can measure our faith at any given time; of having the confidence of knowing *"that in all things God works for the good of those who love Him, who have been called according to His purpose."* (Romans 8:28)

Still, having faith is a tall order when times are tough. If we look back over our lives, and realize how many times God has seen us through the difficult times, how many times He has worked things out for the good, then we can have confidence, faith, trust, that in the future or whatever you may be going through now, He will work things out for your good.

The Triune God

Earlier in the study we identified Jesus as the **Rock**. Here in Isaiah 26:4, however, YAHWEH is designated the "Rock." Is this an example of a so-called "inconsistency" which many unbelievers look for in Scripture to justify their unbelief, or is there a deeper lesson? Are there two "Rocks?" Let's use Scripture to show the true consistency of what on the surface may seem to be inconsistent.

In John 14:6-9 *"Jesus answered, 'I am the Way and the Truth and the Life. No one comes to the Father except through Me. If you really knew Me, you would know My Father as well. From now on, you do know Him and have seen Him.' Phillip said, 'Lord, show us the Father and that will be enough for us.' Jesus answered: 'Don't you know Me, Philip, even after I have been among you for such a long time?* **Anyone who has seen Me has seen the Father.** *How can you say, 'Show us the Father?' Don't you believe that I am in the Father, and the Father is in Me?...'"* In John 10:30, Jesus says *"I and the Father are One."* Hebrews 1:3 says: *"The Son is the radi-*

ance of God's glory and **the exact representation** of His being." These Scriptures indicate that both God the Father and Jesus together, as well as individually, can be the same "Rock."

We have shown previously where *YHVH* (LORD) refers to the Father, and in Isaiah *Adonai* (Lord) refers to Jesus. However, there are times when these two names stand together, side-by-side. When this occurs it is translated as "Sovereign LORD" and represents a compound name of God. In the first chapter of Genesis, God said *"Let **Us** make man in **Our** image, in **Our** likeness…"* (Genesis 1:26a) Obviously, this expresses that God is not singular.

Thus far, this lesson has unintentionally shown that God is at least a dichotomy, a manifestation of two. Throughout the ages, the Church has believed in the "Triune God." Much has been written about the *Trinity*. It has been called a mystery, unscriptural, unknowable. Certainly the finite finds it extremely difficult to understand the **infinite**, but the Apostle Paul gives us a peek in II Corinthians 3:17: *"Now the Lord is the **Spirit**, and where the Spirit of the Lord is, there is freedom."* Paul says that Jesus is the Spirit (that is the Holy Spirit). How can He be both? This transcends the comprehension and wisdom of the finite mind. Paul says Jesus is the Spirit. Jesus said *"Anyone who has seen Me has seen the Father,"* (John 14:9b) and that *"I and the Father are One."* (John 10:20) In Deuteronomy 6:4, we read: *"Hear, O Israel: the LORD our God, the LORD is One."* The LORD is One, but He has the ability to compound Himself, in three manifestations of one substance, known as Father, Son and Holy Spirit. The LORD, the Lord is the Rock. Both collectively and individually, God is One.

Concerning the Resurrection

"Though grace (grace: undeserved kindness, unmerited love from God) *is shown to the wicked, they do not learn righteousness; even in a land of uprightness they go on doing evil and regard not the majesty of the LORD."* (Isaiah 26:10) God is patient, kind, loving and considerate; wanting all men to be saved (I Timothy 2:4; II Peter 3:9), but His patience will not last forever. Some people ask, "How could a kind, loving God condemn and send anybody to hell?" The truth is, He doesn't. God doesn't send anybody to hell. He tells us if we choose not to obey his

laws and commands, choose to not accept Him as God, choose not to accept and believe in His Son Jesus as the Way, the Truth and the Life; the result will be eternal separation from Him. If we choose this path, we automatically choose our fate and send ourselves to hell, through our own actions, choices, unaccountability and rebellion. So don't blame God if that is where you end up.

If we are obedient to God, then ultimately the path of the righteous is level. He establishes peace for us through the Prince of Peace and in Isaiah 26:19, He guarantees our resurrection. God makes it possible, through Christ, if we choose this way, to get to heaven.

King David believed in the resurrection and wrote about it; the Prophet Daniel believed in the resurrection and wrote about it, and Isaiah believed in the resurrection and wrote about it. All of the New Testament writers not only believed in it, most of them witnessed it firsthand and wrote about it. So for any of the Jewish scholars living at the time of Christ there was no excuse for not believing what the Old Testament Scriptures taught about the resurrection. And yet the Sadducees did not believe in the resurrection. That is why they were "sad, you see."

The Corinthians were having a difficult time believing in the resurrection. They were, no doubt, questioning the Apostle Paul about it. Paul answered in I Corinthians 15:1-8. He basically told the Corinthians that if they didn't believe him, then go ask the more than 500 people who saw the resurrected Jesus at the same time. Most of those people were still alive. Go interview them, Corinthians. See if they don't all tell the same story as you question them individually. Paul goes on in verse 13: *"If there is no resurrection of the dead then not even Christ has been raised. And if Christ has not been raised, our preaching is useless and so is your faith."* He continues in verse 19: *"If only for this life we have hope in Christ we are to be pitied more than all men."*

This is the bedrock of our Christian faith. If the resurrection didn't happen, then everything else is trash. Wherever the writers of the New Testament went, they preached the resurrection. That is all they preached; Christ crucified and resurrected. They knew what they saw, and the threat of death—even death itself—could not change the message they preached.

Listen again to Isaiah's confirmation in 26:19. *"But your dead will live; their bodies will rise. You who dwell in the dust, wake up and shout for joy…the earth will give birth to her dead."*

Israel to be Re-established in the Land

Isaiah Chapter 27 has some interesting prophetic promises. Verses 12 and 13 both start out with "in that day." These two verses may not be meant to be chronological, but let's look at them as though they might be. The LORD says in verse 12 that *"…in that day…*(the) *Israelites will be gathered up one by one."* Almost all of the Old Testament prophets point to the end-time regathering, from all over the world, of the scattered nation of Israel. Let's look at a couple of these prophetic promises in Jeremiah as examples. Jeremiah 23:7-8 reads: *"So then, the days are coming, declares the LORD, when people will no longer say, 'As surely as the LORD lives, who brought the Israelites up out of Egypt,' but they will say, 'As surely as the LORD lives, Who brought the descendants of Israel up out of the land of the north and out of all the countries where He had banished them.' Then they will live in their own land."* Again, Jeremiah says in 31:8: *"See, I will bring them from the land of the north and gather them from the ends of the earth. Among them will be the blind and the lame, expectant mothers and women in labor; a great throng will return."*

Returning to Isaiah 27, verse 13 tells us that *"In that day a great trumpet will sound."* Could this be the same trumpet *(shofar)* that calls the scattered, world-wide Church home? We have already seen Israel historically established as a nation in 1948, with great throngs of Jewish people returning to their homeland ever since. At the sound of the trumpet, **all** the Jewish people will be called to their homeland.

Isaiah Chapter 28:15 tells us the people of Jerusalem have entered into a covenant with death, an agreement with the grave. They have made a lie their refuge and falsehood their hiding place. The exact meaning of this may be somewhat obscure. Some believe it is a covenant (a contract or an agreement), with the Antichrist, during the seven-year Tribulation period. Some think it expresses the natural phenomenon of death occurring to all. Either way, Isaiah goes on in verses 16-18 to tell us that the **Precious Cornerstone** (Jesus) will annul this covenant—this contract, this agreement—with death and the grave. Time and time again the promise is made. Death will be done away with forever.

Faith Questions

1. What is Jesus talking about in Matthew 19:28 concerning the "renewal of all things?"
2. How are faith and trust related?
3. Why is the resurrection of Jesus so important to the Christian faith?
4. Do you believe the current nation of Israel is a fulfillment of prophecy? Explain why or why not.

Lesson 15

Isaiah Chapters 29 Through 32
Lip Service is Not Enough

Isaiah Chapter 29 covers a different theme. It is demonstrating, once again, God's displeasure with the worship practices of His people. Verse 13 reads: *"The **Lord** says: 'These people come near to Me with their mouth and honor Me with their lips, but their hearts are far from Me. Their worship of Me is made up only of rules taught by men.'"* Let's carry this thought forward 750 years into the future, to the time of our **Lord** Jesus as recorded in Matthew 15:3-12. *"Jesus replied, 'And why do you break the command of God for the sake of your tradition? For God said, 'Honor your father and your mother' and 'Anyone who curses his father or mother must be put to death.' But you say that if a man says to his father or mother 'Whatever help you might otherwise have received from me is a gift devoted to God,' he is not to 'honor his father with it.' Thus you nullify the Word of God for the sake of your tradition. You hypocrites! Isaiah was right when he prophesied about you: 'These people honor **Me** with their lips, but their hearts are far from **Me.**'"* Jesus is quoting Himself, about Himself. He is the One who told Isaiah this in the first place. He is just affirming that Isaiah got the quote right.

There is another message here concerning our religious traditions. Of course there is nothing wrong with religious traditions, as long as these traditions are rooted and grounded in Scripture. But how many of our religious traditions are not rooted and grounded in Scripture? Upon closer examination, many could be found. The question becomes: which is more important? Which one takes precedence over the other? All denominational traditions should be run through the filter of Holy Scripture. Otherwise we run the risk of our worship being in vain and our teachings being merely rules made up by man. When it came to teaching rules made up by man, hardly anyone outdid the Pharisees. Just like today—no one wants their beliefs and teachings questioned. If you do question them, they will likely be very upset with you. In all the centuries man has been upon the face of the earth, except for the Spirit of God indwelling us, we just haven't changed a bit. Matthew 15:12 reads; *"Then the disciples came to Him and asked, 'Do you know that the Pharisees were offended when they heard this?'"* You should read His reply.

Do we, as Isaiah said, worship the Lord with our lips but have no place in our hearts for Him? Do we have what is known as "head" knowledge, but no "heart" knowledge? With all the different attitudes and beliefs about who God is that are circulating in the world today, even our head knowledge can be questioned.

Prophesy Only Good Things!

Isaiah Chapter 30 continues to recite God's frustration with His children. In verses 9-11, it says: *"These are rebellious people, deceitful children, children unwilling to listen to the LORD's instruction. They say to the seers, 'See no more visions!' And to the prophets, 'Give us no more visions of what is right! Tell us pleasant things, prophesy illusions. Leave this way, get off this path, and stop confronting us with the* **Holy One of Israel***!'"*

Isaiah was not unique concerning people wanting him to only prophesy good things, even if he had to make it up. All of the recorded prophets had this resentment displayed towards them. Many of the prophets were killed because of this hatred of them for being given and repeating God's Word. This form of human behavior, this resistance to the Word of God, cannot change as long as mankind remains in its unregenerate state. Only through Christ and the power of the Holy Spirit can the veil be removed. The Apostle Paul warned Timothy to be aware of this. In II Timothy 4:2-4, Paul wrote: *"Preach the Word; be prepared in season and out of the season; correct, rebuke and encourage with great patience and careful instruction. For the time will come when men will not put up with sound doctrine. Instead, to suit their own desires, they will gather around them a great number of teachers to say what their itching ears want to hear. They will turn their ears away from the truth and turn aside to myths."*

This battle, this struggle, is just as prevalent today as it has ever been. How much pressure is put on our pastors not to bring up and speak about "controversial" issues? How much pressure is put on pastors to give entertaining sermons which have no soul-winning content? How many church councils and/or elder committees instruct pastors not to make anyone uncomfortable? How many church members scold the pastor, saying "Don't tell us about our sins, we don't want to know about hell " Some pastors learned not to do these things at seminary. If they should speak of Satan at all, he is just a figurehead, not someone who would have power to influence people for wrongdoing. Of course, the list goes on.

To compromise God's Word in any way is to not only give the enemy a foothold; it can result in a total surrender to the values of the world. If your goal is advancing and building the Kingdom of God here on earth, then you must not be guilty of compromising and watering down the Word of God. It is nice to be liked, nice to be popular, nice to have the appearance of success, and the appearance of high Scriptural intelligence and wisdom, but not at the expense of compromising God's Word. Isaiah just told us in Chapter 29 that *"the wisdom of the wise will perish, the intelligence of the intelligent will vanish."* (Verse 14:b)

The Arm of the LORD

In the last part of Chapter 30, for the first time, Isaiah uses the word "**arm**." Verse 30 reads: *"The LORD will cause men to hear His **majestic voice** and will make them see His **Arm** coming down…"*

Isaiah speaks here of the "majestic voice." Peter tells us in his second book that he and others heard this voice. In II Peter 1:16-17, we read: *"We did not follow cleverly invented stories when we told you about the power and coming of our Lord Jesus Christ, but we were eyewitnesses of*

*His Majesty. For He received honor and glory from God the Father when the **voice** came to Him saying, 'This is My Son, whom I love; with Him I am well pleased.' We ourselves heard this **voice** that came from heaven when we were with Him on the sacred mountain."* In this example, God the Father caused men to hear His majestic voice. Hearing His voice is associated with seeing His Arm.

What do you think of when you hear the phrase "Arm of God?" Do you see this Arm as part of God's body? Being of one substance? An extension of God Himself? Do we look at it in human terms, as our arm is attached to us? A vital part attached to God? What—or could it be who—is the Arm of God? Verse 30 was not completely quoted above. God the Father said He will cause men to "*see His **Arm** coming down with raging anger and consuming fire, with cloudburst, thunderstorm and hail.*"

Raging anger and consuming fire is synonymous with God's wrath as recorded in Revelation. God's wrath is what takes place during the Tribulation. We know from previous Scriptures we have studied that the whole earth will see Jesus return to culminate history as we know it. Isaiah is saying that men will see God's Arm coming down, and the New Testament writers saying the whole earth will see Jesus coming down, one can only conclude that the "Arm" written of by Isaiah is Jesus. However, by itself, this evidence may be a little weak. So let's flesh it in a little more with Scripture.

Isaiah speaks several times of this "Arm" in the chapters following Chapter 30. As an example, Chapter 51:5 reads: *"My righteousness draws near speedily and My **Salvation** is on the way, and My **Arm** will bring justice to the nations. The islands will look to Me and wait in hope for my **Arm**."* Let's take this verse and do some substitution of the highlighted words. *"My righteousness draws near speedily and My **Jesus** is on the way, and My **Jesus** will bring justice to the nations. The islands* (nations) *will look to Me and wait in hope for My **Jesus**."*

Has the meaning been changed? Has it been corrupted? Or does it seem to fit—logically as well as theologically? Was Jesus on the way when Isaiah wrote this? Yes. Will Jesus bring justice to the nations? Yes. Will the nations hope in Him? Yes!!

We will look at these verses that contain the word "arm" in more detail as we come to them. For the moment though, let's look at Isaiah Chapter 53, because Isaiah 53 identifies this "Arm" of God without any doubt. Verse one begins: *"Who has believed our message and to whom has the **Arm** of the LORD been revealed?"* That is the question. Who has had the Arm of the LORD revealed to them? One thing is certain: this Arm has gender. Isaiah's detailed description of the Arm begins in 53:2, with the personal pronoun **He.** The **Arm** is a He. Isaiah goes on to describe in detail the suffering Messiah's ministry while on earth, which we will study later when we come to Chapter 53. But for right now, we want to point out that the Arm has been revealed to us, the Church. There can be no other association of the Arm of God with anything, or anyone, other than Jesus Christ. We now have a new code word given to us by Isaiah to identify Jesus in his writings. That code word is **Arm.**

How Many Isaiahs?

Many liberal scholars like to divide up the book of Isaiah into little segments. They can then employ their higher critical method, which results in the discrediting of God's Word as recorded in Isaiah. All this is done in the effort to get at the so-called "truth." As mentioned at the beginning of this study, they think they see different writers because Isaiah speaks of different historical times which one man couldn't live long enough to have been able to historically see and record. Therefore, since their god is incapable of knowing the future and imparting that knowledge to men, their reasoning leaves only one possible conclusion. That conclusion is that more than one writer contributed to the book of Isaiah and at a later date, somebody else assembled it under one name.

Multiple writers would not employ the same phrases and code words as one writer would do. The gaps between the times the supposed writers would have written, and their inability to know first-hand what the other writers said and how they said it, flies in the face of the consistency and unity found in Isaiah. In addition—writers being the vain creatures they are—want their names on their own works, not lost under somebody else's name. Therefore, these writers, had they existed, would have made sure their names were prominently displayed with their works for all to see. Phrases like "the Holy One of Israel" and the "Arm of the LORD" cross the theoretical boundaries imposed by these liberal scholars, and therefore help establish the continuity, unity, style and unique way Isaiah was able to distinguish between the Father (LORD) and the Son (Lord) that no other prophet (except King David) was able to do. Only Isaiah saw Jesus' glory and wrote about Him – from the beginning to the end of his book. That could only come from one author, with God as His source.

Returning to Chapter 30 once again, men will hear the voice of the LORD; they will see His **Arm** coming down. In verse 32, the role of this **Arm** is to fight in battle at the end of the Tribulation period. This is precisely the role Jesus fills in Zechariah 14:5 and Revelation 19:11-16. In Revelation 19:13, we read: *"He is dressed in a robe dipped in blood, and His Name is the Word of God. The armies of heaven were following Him, riding on white horses and dressed in fine linen, white and clean. Out of His mouth comes a sharp sword with which to strike down the nations."* Jesus is the Arm!

Trusting Weapons or God

Isaiah 31:1 is a message to the people of Israel in Isaiah's own time. During the time of Isaiah's writing, the neighborhood was starting to get bad. The rulers of Israel were looking for military alliances to help keep stronger nations at bay. God told them they were looking in the wrong place for security. They were putting their trust in the armaments and power of Egypt. Even today, it seems as though America has become the modern-day Egypt the Israelites are relying on. It is certainly very important for America, as a nation, to bless Israel (Genesis 12:3), and stand with them as a friend. But many of America's actions today – such as telling Israel what to do militarily, and strongly urging the division of their God-given land – land for peace – is not blessing them.

God told the Israelites *"Woe to those who go down to Egypt for help, who rely on horses … but do not look to* **the Holy One of Israel**, *or seek help from the* **LORD**.*"* Again, notice there is a distinction between the "Holy One of Israel" and the "LORD." They are made separate by the word "or." The real power for any nation is the Holy One of Israel, and his Father, YHVH the LORD.

History is full of nations and empires that either did not recognize, or else forsook the LORD. Any nation, empire or other form of government, including republics and democracies, that does not acknowledge God, or loses sight of their Godly heritage, will not survive long. History is our witness. If in this country we are starting to trust in and rely on our technology, our armaments, our wealth and our sense of self-reliance, without acknowledging God—that our blessings are a result of His good grace and not our works—then we too will suffer the same consequences as the nations and governments before us.

Moving on to Isaiah 31:5, we read: *"Like birds hovering overhead, the* LORD *Almighty will shield Jerusalem; He will shield it and deliver it, He will '**pass over**' it and rescue it."* Here we have a picture, or a type, of the original Passover experience. During the end times, God will shield Jerusalem from His wrath...it will be "passed over" as His wrath is poured out. We have confirmation of this in Zechariah 12:6. *"On that day I will make the leaders of Judah like a firepot in a woodpile, like a flaming forge among sheaves. They will consume right and left all the surrounding peoples, but Jerusalem will remain intact in her place."* The prophetic promises are very rich in Zechariah 12, 13 and 14. As the reader, you are encouraged to study it carefully. Zechariah says that **all** who come against Jerusalem will hurt themselves. It is all here for the nations to read and understand, if only they would do so!

The Righteous Ruler

Chapter 32 of Isaiah begins by telling us of a King that will rule in righteousness. The only One who could possibly rule in righteousness is Jesus. When He comes to renew all things, each man will be like a shelter from the storm, like streams of water in the desert. Verse 3 implies that at this time the veil and the shroud spoken of in Isaiah 25 shall not be in existence. *"Then the eyes of those who see will no longer be closed, and the ears of those who hear will listen."* Eyes are no longer going to be blinded from the truth. Ears will hear instead of being deaf. Our mothers used to tell us things when we were children, and many times they accused us of having what they said "go in one ear and out the other." For some people, when it comes to God's Word, it goes in one ear, picks up speed, then goes out the other. Isaiah says that at the renewal of all things this will not be the case.

There will be another difference at that time as well. Isaiah 32:5 says: *"No longer will the fool be called noble nor the scoundrel be highly respected."* Having the fool called noble, and the scoundrel, crook, liar, adulterer, and pornographer be highly respected, sends us back to what Isaiah said in Chapter 5. *"Woe to them who call evil good and good evil who put darkness for light and light for darkness."* This will no longer be true at the renewal of all things.

In our society, who do we consider noble and highly respected? Who are our heroes? Unfortunately, it seems to be whoever can hit or kick the ball the farthest, or run with it the fastest. For some, our heroes are on screen, seeing who can take their clothes off the fastest. For a short time after September 11, 2001, we had some sense of who and what real heroes were. But that certainly faded quickly.

Karl Marx once said that "religion is the opiate of the people." Now, one could argue that the sports stadium, the theater, the computer, and even the debased sitcoms on TV have become the opiate of the people. Anything to take our mind off our troubles, to take our mind away from world tensions, or even to soothe our nerves after watching the World Trade Center towers come down. These things help us in re-establishing our complacency. The process of desensitizing continues. The one who lies to us is the one we think is telling us the truth, and the one who tells us the truth we think is lying to us. Satan has this world turned upside down, and only in Christ is the veil taken away.

Faith Questions

1. What is the difference between "lip service" and "heart service?"
2. Why is the Word of God so distasteful to so many?
3. Why is it important to identify "code" words, such as "arm?"
4. Who do you trust: guns, or God? Why?
5. Why is it dangerous for one to call good evil and evil good?

Lesson 16

ISAIAH CHAPTERS 34 THROUGH 40
ALL NATIONS WILL SUFFER

The first four verses of Isaiah Chapter 34 reveal the ultimate judgment against all the nations of the earth. It is specifically time-sensitive to the end days. *"Come near, you nations, and listen; pay attention, you peoples! Let the earth hear, and all that is in it, the world, and all that comes out of it! The* LORD *is angry with all nations; His* **wrath** *is upon all their armies. He will totally destroy them, He will give them over to slaughter."* This compares to Revelation 19:19: *"Then I saw the beast and the kings of the earth and their armies gathered together to make war against the rider on the horse* (Jesus) *and His army."* John the Revelator goes on to explain that Jesus will destroy these armies with the sword that comes out of His mouth—not only the armies, but the nations as well. God's judgment can occur at any time on a person, a nation, or a region. God's wrath is His ultimate in final judgment. His wrath is reserved for special events, most of which have worldwide implications, such as the Flood and the end-times Tribulation. Revelation 6:16-17 was mentioned earlier as the beginning of God's wrath. Daniel 8:19 also dates this wrath as the time of the end. *"He said: 'I'm going to tell you what will happen later in the time of* **wrath***, because the vision concerns the appointed* **time of the**

***end.*'"** Isaiah, Daniel and the Apostle John agree because they had the same source ... God Himself.

Isaiah 34:3 continues: *"Their slain will be thrown out, their dead bodies will send up a stench; the mountains will be soaked with their blood."* Revelation 14:20 indicates that blood will be flowing as high as the horse's bridle. Those of you who have lived in the country know firsthand that as an animal dies, it is not long before it gives off a stench. When that happens it is not long until the buzzards start circling overhead. According to recent documentaries, birds of all types, including carrion and other flesh-eating varieties, are greatly increasing in the land of Israel. The number of birds struck by Israeli aircraft has greatly increased in recent years. Environmentalists would say this is great; the bird ecology is making a comeback. On the surface this appears to be a natural phenomenon. Do you suppose it could have anything to do with preparing for Revelation 19:17 and 21? *"And I saw an angel standing in the sun, who cried in a loud voice to all the birds flying in midair, 'Come, gather together for the great supper of God, so that you may eat the flesh of kings, generals, and mighty men, of horses and their riders, and the flesh of all people; free and slave, small and great'" "...and all the birds gorged themselves on their flesh."*

Isaiah 34:4 reads: *"All the stars of the heavens will be dissolved and the sky rolled up like a scroll; all the starry hosts will fall...."* This compares with Isaiah's previous description in Chapter 13 and with Jesus' description in Matthew 24:29. *"Immediately after the distress of those days the sun will be darkened, and the moon will not give its light; the stars will fall from the sky, and the heavenly bodies will be shaken."*

Zechariah 14:12-15 describes a phenomenon that is specific to intense radiation exposure. *"This is the plague with which the* LORD *will strike all the nations that fought against Jerusalem: Their flesh will rot while they are still standing on their feet, their eyes will rot in their sockets, and their tongues will rot in their mouths. On that day men will be stricken by the* LORD *with great panic. Each man will seize the hand of another, and they will attack each other. Judah too will fight at Jerusalem. The wealth of all the surrounding nations will be collected – great quantities of gold and silver and clothing. A similar plague will strike the horses and mules, the camels and donkeys, and all the animals in those camps."* Although God may use a different means other than radiation, a nuclear exchange would certainly not be out of the realm of possibility. A neutron bomb that kills by radiation alone, but leaves buildings intact, would cause the same symptoms as described in Zechariah.

These prophetic promises were future to Isaiah, future to Zechariah, and future to Jesus' first coming; and are still future to us. It will not be a good time to be living on the earth. Let's hope and pray the Rapture occurs first!

From Wrath to Joy

Isaiah Chapter 35 switches gears from God's wrath to joy. *"The desert and the parched land will be glad; the wilderness will rejoice and blossom. Like the crocus, it will burst into bloom; it will rejoice greatly and shout for joy."*

Samuel Clemens, a.k.a. Mark Twain, traveled to Israel during the late 1800s. He was appalled by what he saw. It was nothing but desert. Nothing was growing there, and very few people were living there. He couldn't imagine why anybody would want to live there or go back to that country. Today, Israel is a major supplier of flowers and fruit to the European Union. The desert has indeed blossomed. It will bloom even more during the Millennial reign of Christ.

God speaks to Isaiah in 35:4-6. *"Say to those with fearful hearts, be strong, do not fear;* **your God will come,** *He will come with vengeance; with divine retribution* **He will come to save you***. Then will the eyes of the blind be opened and the ears of the deaf unstopped. Then will the lame leap like a deer, and the mute tongue shout for joy."* These prophetic promises apply to both the First and Second Comings of Jesus Christ.

When John the Baptist was in prison, he certainly had time on his hands. He had plenty of time to think and to look back over his ministry. Imprisoned for his faith, he had opportunity to question his beliefs. He might have thought, "Why would God do this to me? I was busy working, spreading the gospel. God should have prevented this." John was even questioning whether Jesus was truly the Messiah, or should he look for someone else? We pick up the commentary in Matthew 11:2: *"When John heard in prison what Christ was doing, he sent his disciples to ask Him, 'Are you the One who was to come, or should we expect someone* else?' Jesus replied, 'Go back and report to John what you hear and see: The blind receive sight, the lame walk, those who have leprosy are cured, the deaf hear, the dead are raised, and the good news is preached to the poor.'"*

Jesus did not send the message back that He was the Son of God. He did not say He was the Messiah. Anyone could identify himself as the Messiah, but that did not mean it was so. Many had come before Jesus and many came after Him, claiming to be the Messiah. Instead, through John's disciples, Jesus told John to look at the evidence; to look at the fruit of His labor, and compare it to what the Scripture said would be the works that accompanied the coming of the Messiah.

John knew, based in large part on Isaiah's teaching, that when the real, true Messiah came He would cause the eyes of the blind to be opened, the ears of the deaf to hear, and the lame to walk. He also knew of other Scripture which said the Messiah would raise the dead and preach the Good News to the poor. John knew most of these signs could not be faked, that only the real Messiah could perform them. When John heard what Jesus was doing, it no doubt gave great comfort and peace of mind to his heart and spirit.

Similar conditions will again exist at the Second Coming. There will be physical healing, as well as spiritual healing when the veil is removed, allowing the spiritually blind and deaf to see and hear the truth.

Isaiah Chapters 36 through 39 are part of the account related in an earlier lesson concerning King Hezekiah of Judah and King Sennacherib of Assyria.

An Awesome Chapter; An Awesome God!

Isaiah Chapter 40 is one of those chapters that cover a lot of different topics. It is an awesome chapter, giving us awesome insight into an awesome God. Verse 3 is a prophetic promise concerning the ministry of John the Baptist: *"A voice of one calling: 'In the desert prepare the way for the LORD; make straight in the wilderness a highway for our God.'"* The New Testament book of Mark testifies this verse is a prophecy concerning John the Baptist. Mark 1:3 says: *"A voice of one calling in the desert, 'Prepare the way for the Lord, make straight paths for Him.' And so John came, baptizing in the desert region and preaching a baptism of repentance for the forgiveness of sins."* John the Baptist did indeed make straight a highway for God, Who became flesh and dwelt among us for awhile.

Isaiah 40:10-11 again identifies the Arm of the LORD. Whereas Isaiah's first identification of the Arm had to do with the **Lord** leading an army with wrath and consuming fire, this time Isaiah identifies Him as King and Shepherd. *"See, the Sovereign LORD comes with power, and His **Arm rules** for Him. See, His reward is with Him, and His recompense accompanies Him. He tends His flock like a **shepherd**: He gathers the lambs in His arms and carries them close to His heart; He gently leads those that have young."* The Sovereign LORD is the compound name for God, as previously talked about. The fact that the **Arm** rules for Him makes Him King. He will be a good King, not a tyrant. Even as King, the supreme ultimate authority, He will have the servant heart of a shepherd.

Was Jesus the good Shepherd while He was on earth the first time? There is a good test that can be used to determine if Jesus, or any of His pastors, elders, or deacons are good shepherds. Ask this question: Whose best interest does the shepherd always have at heart? His, or others? The answer to this question will determine where any "shepherd," or even you personally, are on this scale. Jesus always placed everyone else's best interests above His own. After all, Jesus (being God) wants all men to be saved (I Timothy 2:4, II Peter 3:9).

In the first 16 verses of John Chapter 10, Jesus goes into great detail in describing the attributes of a good shepherd. *"I am the good Shepherd..."* Jesus said, and in verse 15, He said *"...and I will lay down My life for the sheep."* This is the ultimate in placing others ahead of you.

Trying to Understand Why

Isaiah 40:14 to the end of the chapter is somewhat reminiscent of Job Chapter 38. Job had been asking "why" questions, and had been making statements that seemed wise to him, but were way down on the scale of intelligence compared to God. God very seldom answers "why" questions, and He never answers "how" questions. God never tells us how He created heaven and earth. He doesn't tell us how He makes the laws of physics work, and He doesn't answer Job's "why" questions.

Job didn't have Job Chapters 1 and 2 to tell him what was going on. These chapters are one of very few cases in which God answers "why."

God tells us that good can come out of tragic events, but never why we or our loved ones have to go through them. These tragic events are almost always accompanied by spiritual growth, which is recognizable once one gets through it.

When God tired of Job's "why" questions, He answered Job in Chapter 38 from a position of His power, majesty, and awesomeness. With His superior intelligence and knowledge, God began to ask Job questions. *"Where were you when I laid the earth's foundation?" "Can you bring forth the constellations in their seasons…?" "Do you know the laws of the heavens?" "Who endowed the heart with wisdom or gave understanding to the mind?"* These are just a few of the many questions God asked Job, of which Job could answer none. We could do little better, even with our increased scientific knowledge.

The questions continue in Isaiah 40:13-14: *"Who has understood the mind (Spirit) of the LORD, or instructed Him as His counselor? Whom did the LORD consult to enlighten Him, and who taught Him the right way? Who was it that taught Him knowledge or showed Him the path of understanding?"* Are you feeling "intelligently insignificant" yet?

Creation or Evolution?

In the above verses, God is basically asking man: Where did his "knowledge," which is information, come from? The following discussion may at first seem a little off the topic of knowledge and information, but God's topic of creation continues with the rest of Isaiah Chapter 40.

Let's talk about the logic in the creation versus evolution debate, and the question about information and its origin. Perhaps this discussion will help you with your apologetics of defending God and His Word.

When making logical statements, sometimes a simple demonstration everyone can understand is in order. This simple demonstration begins like this: If you look at a mousetrap, you'll see it has nine components to it, each component meticulously designed with a specific function. Taken as a whole, with all parts working together for the desired result, it will do what it was designed to do: catch mice. However, remove just one of its components and it will no longer function. In scientific circles this is called "irreducible complexity"—in this case, meaning anything less than nine components renders it useless.

A single cell from the simplest life form has about 300 components. What goes on inside the cell is overwhelmingly complex and is yet to be fully understood. What science does know is each component has a specific function, and it works in conjunction with all the other components, producing the desired result. In the case of this single cell, the desired result is to gather and process food into energy, then be able to exactly reproduce itself and pass along digital information contained in its DNA, which is no simple task. It is extremely complex.

Science tells us these 300 or so components that made up the first living cell came together by chance happening; by purposeless, natural processes. Life came from non-life…life from lifeless rocks, chemicals, energy and whatever else that might be needed to produce this first living cell. This is known in science as "chemical evolution" and the process is known as "self-organization." This is all considered a "natural" process, not supernatural. The natural process is the only one science will consider. This supposedly all happened over millions (or perhaps billions) of years, in the so-called "primordial soup" of early planet earth.

Science should be able to show the empirical evidence that proves their theory is the correct one: evidence that can be observed, tested, controlled and duplicated in a controlled environment such as a laboratory. Let science create life! Let them put all the ingredients they claim to know were present in the "primordial soup" together. Realizing primitive earth did not have ideal, controlled conditions, and the primordial soup was probably contaminated, this project of creating life should be a snap.

As a matter of fact, this has been tried thousands of times since it was first attempted in the 1950s, all without success. Modern human beings, intelligent creatures that we are, have been unable under the most ideal and controlled conditions to produce a single cell of life from scratch. No one would believe the mousetrap came into existence by accident, no matter how much time it had to self-assemble or self-organize. If science can't produce life with all of its laboratory sophistication, then how can they expect people to believe evolution's theory that a single cell of life, which is infinitely more complex than a mousetrap, came into being by accident, by chance happening?

You see, if there is no God, then there is no creation! If there is no God, there are no miracles. If there is no God, then life was just a chance happening. If there is no God, scientists have to keep looking for the missing evidence where life first crawled out of the ocean. "From goo to you by way of the zoo" is what they want you to believe. If scientists discard the possibility of the supernatural, they will come up with new theories, looking for that "missing link" until the end of time. *"They are always learning but never able to acknowledge the truth."* (II Timothy 3:7) This attitude also exposes what the majority of scientists really believe about God: that there is no God. Therefore, they must keep on searching for the proof they feel must exist about how and when life started by accident, by chance happening.

The probabilities of chemicals self-assembling into the simplest living cell have been calculated as 1 in 10 to the 100 billionth power (*Origins, A Skeptic's Guide to the Creation of Life on Earth;* Robert Shapiro; New York: Summit Books, 1986; page 128). That is a "1" with 100 billion zeros behind it. God said He created the earth in six days. For many of you, God said it and that is the end of the matter; for others this is a stumbling block. With these kinds of odds, it doesn't matter whether the cosmos is six seconds, 6,000 years, or 15 billion years old; it is magnitudes of power too young for life to have a chance at self-assembly when the odds are 1 in 10 to the 100 billionth power. It also doesn't matter how many earth-like planets some scientists think may be out there. You might want to remind your secular friends of this.

There are two theories among Bible-believing Christians concerning how long ago God created the earth. One camp is described as "young earth," the other as "old earth." Both sides will cite Scripture and original Hebrew word meanings, along with scientific evidence, to persuade other believers as to which theory is Biblically-correct. These groups will go at each other in a manner that is sometimes not very loving; even calling into question the opposing side's salvation. As stated above by the statistical mathematicians, it took an act of God to bring about the creation of the cosmos, no matter how old it may be. When speaking to highly-educated non-believers, especially those of scientific persuasion, do not start out acknowledging a belief that the earth is only 6,000 years old, or some other early age. This is an immediate turn-off for them, and nothing else you may say concerning the Bible after that will have any credibility with them. The opportunity to witness to them will be lost.

The goal of these conversations is to plant the seed that God will then use to turn unbelievers into believers. We should not make our belief that the earth is a specific age the litmus test for becoming a believer. Don't be dogmatic on first contact; but with love, allow the possibility for an older age. Our salvation comes through Jesus Christ and His shed blood, not in knowing the exact age of the earth. If God wanted us to know the exact age, He would have told us plainly. Allow the Holy Spirit to work by not insisting on an issue that does not have a bearing on salvation.

You certainly can discuss these issues among believers, but do not make it an issue with highly-educated unbelievers. Instead, point to the overwhelming evidence in favor of design and complexity, and the things that couldn't have possibly happened by chance. If you don't want to lose them, let them become believers first. Then, if you must, discuss the age of the universe. The point is, it is unfruitful for Christians to argue the age of the earth, especially when it is not a salvation issue. Not many minds among Christians have been changed as result of these sometimes heated debates. What has happened is a lot of animosity, and hard feelings. And isn't that just what the enemy wants? Let's not fall prey to the enemy on this issue.

It has also been circulated that life on earth was seeded here by some unknown unidentified extraterrestrials from some distant galaxy. This is an attempt by some unbelieving scientists to explain away the creative evidence that points to God. They will explore every avenue possible, even when there is absolutely no evidence to support their theory, in their attempt to run away from God and deny Him and His existence. Denying the existence of God is really what it is all about. Besides having absolutely no evidence concerning extraterrestrials, we need to keep in mind the laws of physics and the odds against the self-assembly of a single simple cell would apply to any other life form in the cosmos, just as it applies to us. The cosmos is simply not old enough for life to self-assemble, let alone the total improbability of intelligent life evolving naturally.

There are many books written by reputable scientists who are challenging with scientific evidence the theory of self-assembly and evolution. The scientific evidence is beginning to be overwhelmingly in favor of God being the only answer to account for the huge amount of complexity of design and diversity of life that is observed on earth and in the universe.

Let's get back to the concept of information. DNA, which stores huge amounts of information, is itself material with mass. However, information is neither mass nor energy. Everything in the whole universe, in the whole cosmos, is either mass or energy, but information is neither. Let's repeat this: information is neither mass nor energy! Each cell in humans, and all other life forms, contains a digitally-coded database larger in information content than all volumes of a popular encyclopedia. Where did this information come from? Remove any one of 300 components, and the cell stops functioning; the living cell dies. Like the mousetrap, it is irreducibly complex.

This "original" information is outside the bounds and apart from the laws of physics, which govern the entire universe. It had to come from somewhere outside of the physical universe, because it is neither mass nor energy. You can ask any Ph.D. in the sciences; they will not be able to answer where this original information came from. Most will, however, try to get you off the subject with questions of their own. Don't allow them to do that; always keep this question in front of them. That this original information came from God is the only logical conclusion we can draw. This concept is known as "Intelligent Design." The term Intelligent Design raises red flags in the secular world as a "backdoor approach" to introduce religion. Maybe a change is in order. How about calling it "evidence-based education," and let the evidence lead where it may? Who could deny that kind of intellectual honesty?

Going back to the original question: Where did God get His knowledge and information? Job didn't know, Isaiah couldn't figure it out, and people today would rather say God doesn't exist. Avoidance – that is one way to deal with the unknowable answers. Just stick our heads in the sand and all will be well. God is eternal, without beginning or end, and our finite minds are just incapable of knowing more. God doesn't answer "how," and even if He did, we probably wouldn't understand.

In Isaiah 40:22, God gives Isaiah a glimpse into some information that mankind could not confirm until the 1500's. The information was that the earth is round, not flat. *"He* (God) *sits enthroned above the **circle** of the earth."* There is no way Isaiah could have known that, and it went against the popular concept of his time.

Since Isaiah is beginning to open up the subject of creation here and in chapters following, and of Who created the heavens and the earth, we will focus on that topic and try to gain a better understanding. Isaiah 40:26 reads: *"Lift your eyes and look to the heavens: Who created all these? He who brings out the starry hosts one by one, and calls them each by name. Because of His great power and mighty strength, not one of them is missing."* In verse 28, we read: *"Do you not know? Have you not heard? The* LORD *is the everlasting God, the Creator of the ends of the earth...."* Then, in Isaiah 45, verses 12 and 18, God is speaking: *"It is I who made the earth and created mankind upon it. My own hands stretched out the heavens; I marshaled their starry hosts."* ... *"For this is what the* LORD *says—He who created the heavens, He is God; He who fashioned and made the earth, He founded it; He did not create it to be empty, but formed it to be inhabited."*

There is no doubt God created everything, visible and invisible. Science has now concluded that everything in the cosmos did indeed have a beginning, and all matter and energy that is contained in the cosmos was compacted into a space infinitesimally smaller than the period at the end of this sentence. That is incomprehensible. Science then tells us that a huge explosion occurred in that infinitesimally small space, to become what we know as the heavens and the earth. They have dubbed it the "big bang." Many Christians have a problem with this theory. Some reject it outright. For this author, it is not a problem. God spoke the word, and "bang," it happened! However it happened, it is the product of a supernaturally-intelligent Designer, outside the bounds of the physical universe, whom we know as God.

Many microbiologists, astrophysicists (those who study the cosmos) and others have come to faith because of their studies, observations, and conclusions. They came to faith with help from the Holy Spirit, based in part on the scientific evidence uncovered by their studies.

They followed the evidence trail to God. They recognize that the cosmos is so fine-tuned that if any one of the 70 or so currently-known, finely-tuned parameters was even just slightly out of a narrowly-defined range, life as we know it could not exist on earth. They know that the probabilities of these parameters occurring by chance are so great that they are mathematically impossible. In fact, they have concluded that if any small part of the entire cosmos had been missing, that it would have thrown off some of the finely-tuned parameters and life on earth would not and could not exist.

Think of it: God had to put every star, every constellation in the proper numbers and mass for you to have a compatible home environment (planet earth) that was tailor-made for you and your well-being. Planet earth is so complex it can only be one-of-a-kind. Everything in the night sky is there by design. It exists in its entirety to sustain and maintain the earth. Everything had to be, and has to be, just as it was, and is, for you to exist. It exists so you can exist. These scientists' conclusion is that there must have been an outside Intelligence manipulating the events, a Creator. After studying all of the holy books of the world, these scientists found only the God of the Bible and His written Word possessed and showed its supernatural origin. Repeating Isaiah 45:18: *"For this is what the* LORD *says—He who created the heavens, He is God; He who formed and made the earth, He founded it; He did not create it to be empty,* **but formed it to be inhabited***."*

As mentioned before, within this nation there is a debate as to whether Intelligent Design should be taught alongside evolution in high schools. The proponents of "separation of church and state" reject this proposal as tantamount to teaching God in the classroom. We should drop the Intelligent Design label and call for "evidence-based education." Who could object to evidence being provided to our children? In light of the evidence provided so far (and we have only barely scratched the surface), we can just follow the evidence trail to where it leads. It will not lead to Darwin.

In the New Testament the creation event is attributable to Jesus Christ. In John 1:1 we read: *"In the beginning was the Word, and the Word was with God, and the Word was God. He was with God in the beginning. Through Him* **all** *things were made; without Him nothing was* *made that has been made."* The Apostle Paul's letter to the Colossians leaves no doubt as to Who did the creating. Speaking of Jesus, Paul says in Colossians 1:16-17: *"For by Him **all** things were created: things in heaven and on earth, visible and invisible, whether thrones or powers or rulers or authorities; **all** things were created by Him and for Him. He is **before all** things, and in Him **all** things hold together."*

Isaiah attributes the creation to God the Father. John and Paul attribute the creation to Jesus. Is there a conflict here? Let's try to rationalize this. We'll use some Scripture, and see what kind of apologetics we can come up with. First of all, as has been previously demonstrated, if you have seen Jesus you have seen the Father. *"I and the Father are One."* (John 10:30) *"God was pleased to have all His fullness dwell in Him."* (Colossians 1:19) As Hebrews Chapter 1 expresses it: *"The Son is the radiance of God's glory and the **exact** representation of His being...."* They are one substance.

If you and your family decide to build a house, you would go out and choose a lot in the neighborhood of your choice. You would then more than likely contact a builder, choose a house plan, and commission him to start as soon as possible. After the house is built, a friend of yours drives down the street with a carload of his friends. He says to them, "This is the house that my friend and his spouse built." Would this be a true statement? Did you and your spouse build the house, or did the contractor? Both of those statements would be true. The contractor, along with you and your spouse, each had a role in the building of this house. This brings us back to the question of Who created the heavens and the earth—the Father or the Son? There is more light shed on this question in Proverbs Chapter 8.

Proverbs Chapter 8 starts out as a personification of wisdom. But midway through, the subjective, inanimate subject of wisdom begins to take on the Deistic qualities that are attributable only to Jesus. As an example, in verse 17, it says: *"I love those who love Me..."* Compare that to John 14:21: *"Whoever has My commands and obeys them, he is the one who loves Me. He who loves Me will be loved by My Father and I too will love him and show Myself to him."* Proverbs 8:17 continues: *"...and those who **seek** Me find Me."* Acts 17:26-27 says God *"determined that men should inhabit the whole earth and that He set the times and the exact places* *where they should live. He did this so that men would **seek** Him and perhaps reach out for Him and find Him."* If we would take Proverbs 8:17 at face value, it would seem only to say those who seek wisdom find wisdom. But we know that if you truly seek God, you'll find Him, and thus He imparts to us His Godly wisdom as we are able to receive it.

It is About the Savior

The verses in Proverbs Chapter 8 which are highlighted next can only apply to Jesus and can never apply to wisdom. Verses 22-27 state, in part: *"The LORD brought **Me** forth as the first of His works, before His deeds of old; **I was appointed from eternity, from the beginning, before the world began.** When there were no oceans, **I was** given **birth**... **I was** there when He set the heavens in place."* Skipping to verse 30, we read: *"Then **I was** the **craftsman** at His side. **I was** filled with delight day after day, rejoicing always in His presence..."* Then in verses 32-36, the Speaker says: *"Now then, My sons, listen to **Me**; **blessed are those who keep My ways**. Listen to My instruction and be wise; do not ignore it. Blessed is the man who listens to **Me**, **watching daily at My doors, waiting at My doorway**.* (Compare John 10:9) *For whoever finds **Me** finds **life*** (compare John 14:6) *and receives favor from the LORD. But **whoever fails to find Me harms himself; all who hate Me love death**."*

The "I was" statements, and the "Me" identifications given above are personal pronouns. Personal pronouns are used to express a distinction of persons. Wisdom is not a person! The only way this can fit is to know that Jesus is the embodiment of wisdom. The last verse, verse 36, says *"...whoever finds Me finds life..."* If this whole chapter was talking only about normal wisdom, then we would know that it would be incorrect, because wisdom never possesses deistic qualities. Wisdom cannot impart eternal life; only God can. If it is not talking about natural earthly wisdom, then what other entity completely and fully meets the requirements described here?

Wisdom never has, and never will, **save** anybody. Only Jesus provides salvation through His sacrifice on the cross. Only Jesus was given birth, instead of being created. Only Jesus is from eternity, from everlasting to everlasting. Only Jesus was the **craftsman** at the side of His Father. Jesus is the only One who can truly bless us, if we listen to Him.

Jesus Himself instructs us in Matthew 24 to *"keep watch because you do not know on what day your Lord will come...."* So you also must be ready, because *"the Son of Man will come at an hour when you do not expect Him."* We are to be **"watching daily at (His) doors, waiting at (His) doorway."** (Proverbs 8:34)

We don't want to leave out the role of the Holy Spirit in this creation narrative. Genesis tells us the Spirit of God was over the waters in the very first verse of the creation story. So Who created the heavens and the earth? God the Father? God the Son? God the Holy Spirit? We can only say, yes, They/He did!

Faith Questions

1. Why is there such agreement in prophecy across all books of the Bible?
2. What conditions stand out to you most concerning end times?
3. Why didn't Jesus tell John the Baptist plainly that He was the promised Savior?
4. Is the creation narrative in this chapter enlightening or confusing?

Lesson 17

ISAIAH CHAPTERS 41 AND 42
THE ALPHA AND OMEGA

In Isaiah 41:4, the verse ends: *"I, the* LORD *(God the Father)—with the first of them and with the last—I am He."* Jesus calls Himself the "first and the last" *(Alpha and Omega)* in Revelation 22:13. Are there two "firsts and lasts?" Can two or more persons occupy the same space at the same time? This is logically and physically impossible, but not spiritually impossible. Spiritually speaking, two or more objects can occupy the same space at the same time and still be stand-alone entities, while having the ability to be simultaneously anywhere and everywhere in the physical universe. We, the physical, think in reference to our physical limitations and we try to impose those limitations on the Spiritual realm. God has no limitations: *"…with God all things are possible."* (Matthew 19:26)

Jesus said, *"I and the Father are One."* (John 10:30) This is physically impossible, but not spiritually impossible. God is Spirit, according to John 4:24, and by default so was Jesus in His pre-incarnate state. In Isaiah 43:10, God uses the same "I am He" phrase to identify Himself, just as He did in 41:4.

God first uses the "I AM" phrase in Exodus 3:14. It means "I am He that exists" and "One Who is always present." This would certainly apply to Jesus. (See John 8:58.)

In the book of John, John gives the details of Jesus' arrest in Chapter 18. Intent on arresting Jesus, the mob of soldiers and officials of the priests and Pharisees went up the Mount of Olives carrying torches, lanterns and weapons. We pick up the narrative starting in verse 4: *"Jesus, knowing all that was going to happen to Him, went out and asked them, 'Who is it you want?' 'Jesus of Nazareth,' they replied.* **'I am He***,' Jesus said. When Jesus said, 'I am He' they drew back and fell to the ground."* There wasn't any doubt in the minds of the mob, at that moment, who Jesus was identifying Himself as. Although it is not recorded, Jesus probably spoke this phrase "I am He" in such a thunderous way that those there to arrest Him were absolutely sure they heard the voice of God…and in fact they did. Nothing else can explain why they drew back and fell to the ground.

Remember how Ezekiel, in his vision, the priests who were dedicating the first temple, and also the Apostle John, fell to the ground when they caught a glimpse of Jesus and His glory? This might have happened for a brief moment to the mob that came to arrest Jesus. They certainly reacted in the same manner. Jesus tells us in John 8:58, *"Before Abraham was born, I am!"*

The Promise to Restore Israel

Isaiah 41:8-20 tells God's promises to restore Israel. Keep in mind when Isaiah prophesied this, the nation of Israel was still a powerful nation. It had strong military alliances with Egypt. This self-proclaimed country bumpkin prophet was talking about the people being forcefully scattered to the far corners of the earth, so that at some future time God could bring them back again. Isaiah's contemporaries had to think "Is this guy insane, or what?" The vast majority of people in Isaiah's time, or any of the other prophets' times (including Jesus, the Messiah), did not believe their messages. There can be safety in numbers, but we need to be careful about having a "herd" mentality. When it comes to spiritual matters the "secular herd" will lead you in the wrong direction.

Jesus' True Identity Could Not be Mistaken

Beginning in Isaiah Chapter 42 and including Chapters 49, 50, 52, and 53, we have the beginning of what is known as the "Servant" chapters. These chapters are overwhelmingly full of the identity, suffering, and mission work of Jesus Christ. His sinless nature, His resurrection and work go magnitudes beyond any man's capabilities. In many ways, these chapters have more details concerning the earthly life and ministry of Jesus Christ than what is recorded in the New Testament.

The Apostle John knew and wrote about Jesus; Isaiah saw Jesus' glory and spoke about Him. Isaiah wrote about Jesus and His glory in the preceding chapters already covered in his book, and he continues to do so in the remaining ones, especially in the Servant chapters.

When John the Baptist inquired as to whether Jesus was the one God had promised Who would bring salvation, or if they should look for another, Jesus didn't say "yes" or "no," but instead told John to look at the evidence. Jesus had turned water into wine. He healed every disease and sickness among the people throughout Galilee. He taught people about how those who are pure in heart will be blessed. He taught about giving to the needy, and not judging others. He taught how to discern between good men and evil men by their fruits. He brought a little girl who had died back to life, along with the evidence of how much He taught the people with an authority and power they had never heard before. He performed miracle after miracle, healing after healing. In John 21:25, John tells us: *"Jesus did many other things as well. If every one of them were written down, I suppose that even the whole world would not have room for the books that would be written."* This, then, was the evidence that Jesus sent back to John the Baptist. This evidence was so visible that no one living at that time in Israel could escape it.

In John Chapter 7, as Jesus was teaching during the Feast of Tabernacles, the Jews asked Him a question in verse 15: *"The Jews were amazed and asked, 'How did this man get such learning without having studied?"* Again, in verse 31, they asked: *"When the Christ comes, will He do more miraculous signs than this man?"* The evidence was there. All of the signs that would accompany the Messiah were previously recorded in Isaiah and by other prophets. The Pharisees were jealous, even to the point of murder, because of Jesus' infinitely greater knowledge and wisdom. He was a threat to their authority and power base. One can see quite readily which is most important; power or truth. Most people, if they have to decide between power or truth, will choose power: power over morality, power over honesty, power over preserving life.

Just Look at the Evidence

Jesus said in Matthew 7:20: *"Thus, by their fruits you will recognize them."* Jesus' fruit was plain and visible for all to see. He didn't have to tell people He was the Messiah, because the evidence of His fruit was undeniable in identifying who He truly was. The Jewish people at that time were without excuse. Because of their lack of understanding and accurate knowledge of God, they didn't recognize the time of God's coming to them. A veil covers their eyes, but it will soon be lifted at the Second Coming. For some Jewish believers, the veil has already been removed.

Liberal scholars claim multiple Isaiahs, claiming an eyewitness to the Babylonian conquest recorded what happened and inserted it into the book of Isaiah. What observer do they claim lived at the time of Christ and inserted these historical details into Isaiah? What eyewitness was there in 1948, when Israel was restored as a nation, when the country was *"born in one day?"* (Isaiah 66:8b) The truth is, the eyewitness in 1948 is the same eyewitness of the Babylonian conquest. It was our awesome, all-knowing, all-seeing God.

The Jewish people have always claimed that Isaiah Chapter 53 was inserted by the Christians; that is, until the Dead Sea Scrolls were unearthed in 1947 in Israel. The complete book of Isaiah was found in the Dead Sea Scrolls—and that includes Chapter 53. It was not inserted by Christians. Let's look at the details recorded about Jesus that only God could have given to Isaiah, 750 years before the beginning of their literal fulfillment.

As we start into the Servant chapters, understand that there are two "servants" recorded here. There are the prophetic promises concerning God's Servant Jesus, who in all cases is victorious. God sometimes calls the nation of Israel His servant. This servant has always failed Him, fallen short and let Him down … sort of like us. We will be concentrating and focusing only on the Servant Messiah, Yeshua.

Jesus is Introduced

As Isaiah begins to reveal God's Servant here in Chapter 42, he begins with a formal introduction. If you were employed in the corporate world in a high position of authority, and you were bringing a highly-touted person into a key position, you would first introduce him to key staff members. This introduction would include his name, educational background, previous experience, areas of expertise, assigned duties in this new position and what could be expected from him. You would then sit back and see if he performs up to expectations. It is no different with God when He introduces His Servant Son. God starts out: *"Here is My Servant, whom I uphold, my Chosen One in Whom I delight."* What follows in this chapter, as well as the other aforementioned Servant chapters, are His duties and responsibilities to God and to all of mankind. This includes His mission, and all of the things He will have to go through to accomplish all the tasks set before Him. All we have to do is to watch and see if He performs as promised. If He does (and He has), we can trust Him. We can put our faith in Him, knowing that He is not only the right man for the job; He is the only man for the job.

Verse 1 then begins to show what we can expect of the Servant and what part of His mission will be. *"I will put my Spirit on Him and He will bring justice to the nations. He will not shout or cry out, or raise His voice in the streets."* Isaiah 53:7 acknowledges the same thing about the Suffering Servant. *"He was oppressed and afflicted, yet He did not open His mouth; He was led like a lamb to the slaughter, and as a sheep before her shearers is silent, so He did not open His mouth."* Matthew records in Chapter 26:62, when Jesus was standing accused in front of the Sanhedrin and the high priest, *"Then the high priest stood up and said to Jesus, 'Are You not going to answer? What is this testimony that these men are bringing against You?' But Jesus **remained silent**."*

Isaiah continues in 42:3: *"A bruised reed He will not break, and a smoldering wick He will not snuff out. In faithfulness He will bring forth justice; He will not falter or be discouraged till He establishes justice on earth. In His law the islands* (nations) *will put their hope."* Matthew 12:15-21 quotes these passages and gives affirmation that they were written about Jesus.

Isaiah 42:6 says: *"I, the* LORD, *have called You in righteousness; I will take hold of Your hand. I will keep You and will make You to be a covenant for the people and a Light for the Gentiles."* Jesus is the only one who was born in righteousness and lived in total righteousness. Jesus was to be the Covenant. This covenant, an agreement between God and man for the salvation of mankind, was to be signed with Jesus' sacrificial blood. This was God's handwritten signature that He would not go back on the covenant agreement, or His Word. In Matthew 26:27 we read: *"Then He took the cup, gave thanks and offered it to them, saying, 'Drink from it, all of you. This is My blood of the* **covenant***, which is poured out for many for the forgiveness of sins.'"* This **covenant** agreement, then, is that God will forgive our sins. Our part of the bargain is, when we acknowledge and confess Him and His Son as Lord and Savior, we gain salvation; His sacrificial death for our life. We definitely got the better end of the bargain!

Isaiah 42:6 continues that Jesus would be *"a Light for the Gentiles,"* which is reminiscent of Isaiah Chapter 9 and was covered in an earlier section. Verse 7 is reminiscent of Chapter 35:5-6 where John the Baptist, sitting in a dungeon, made inquiry of the Lord. The answer John received from Jesus certainly gave him mental and spiritual release from the dark dungeon in which he was sitting.

Faith Questions

1. What does it mean when Jesus says He is the "Alpha and Omega?"
2. Why should it have been impossible for people not to recognize who Jesus really was when He came?

Lesson 18

Isaiah Chapters 43 Through 45
There is No Other God

In Isaiah Chapter 43, God the Father uses some of the same descriptive words for Himself that have also been used of Jesus. Examples of this are "I am He," "Savior," "Holy One," "Israel's Creator," "your King." Referencing Hebrews 1:3 is the only way this can be explained.

This chapter in Isaiah is very forthright and explicit in letting the Israelites know there is no other God. There is nowhere else or anybody else they can turn to. In John 6:68, after Jesus asked the 12 disciples if they wanted to leave, too, after many other disciples had stopped following Him, even Peter confessed: *"Simon Peter answered Him, 'Lord, to whom shall we go? You have the words of eternal life. We believe and know that you are the Holy One of God.'"* Peter understood there was no other place to go. There was no other god he (or anyone) could turn to. The sooner mankind figures this out, the better off we will all be. Oh, what a paradise this earth will be, when what is left of the human race after the Tribulation figures this out and worships the one true God!

God challenges the Israelites to go throughout the nations and see if they can find any other god or gods who have had the ability to foretell and proclaim the events that have taken place, and will take place. In speaking of His servant Israel, God says in 43:10: *"'You are my witnesses,' declares the* LORD, *'and My servant whom I have chosen, so that you may know and believe Me and understand that **I am He**.'"* Israel was to be a witness of God's power and glory to the nations—that He was and is the only God. It was true in Isaiah's time, it has been true throughout the centuries, and it is blatantly true today, though the nations are blind to that fact.

All the prophetic promises concerning Jesus that have been fulfilled, and all the prophetic promises concerning the nation of Israel that have been fulfilled, serve as an historic witness to all the world. Even the prophetic promises God made throughout all of the prophetical books, concerning the re-establishment of Israel as a nation after having been dispersed for 2,000 years, serve as a witness to the world. The catastrophic events that have happened to Israel and the Jewish people throughout the centuries are just as God said it would be if they rejected Him. Even the earliest writings from the Prophet Moses, found in Deuteronomy Chapter 28, give in detail the chronological order of events concerning the curses (consequences) that would follow for being disobedient to God. (And they were disobedient!) Deuteronomy Chapter 28 is a microcosm, or encapsulation, of Jewish history that begins with the period of the Judges.

Ancient Israel's Prophetic Future

The first 14 verses of Deuteronomy Chapter 28 express how God will bless the Israelites in their new promised land, if they just carefully follow and obey the LORD. The rest of the chapter outlines to the Jewish people the consequences of disobedience to God. Even today, there can be consequences for us for not being obedient to God.

Let's look at Deuteronomy Chapter 28. It is broken down into six segments, beginning in verse 15. A seventh segment occurs in the first five verses of Chapter 30. The first segment is the time of the Judges. Verses 15 through 31 foretell conditions that would be prevalent during the time of the Judges. Verses 32 through 35 foretell conditions that would be prevalent during the Assyrian captivity.

The third segment is the Babylonian captivity, and it is found in verses 36 and 37. After the Babylonian captivity, Persian King Cyrus allowed all of the nations that had been taken captive to return to their

There is No Other God

homeland. This included the Jewish people. Even though they were allowed to return, they still remained a vassal state under the Medes and Persians, followed by the conquest of Alexander the Great and his empire. Verses 38 through 48, the fourth segment, recount the conditions during the period they were a vassal state. Some of the conditions listed in each of the epochs of time or divisions of Jewish history are common to all, but some conditions are much more dominant during certain historical periods than others. Thus, we are able to separate in the prophetic promises the recognizable divisions of historical events based on recorded history.

The fifth segment, the period of the Roman Empire, begins at verse 49 and continues through verse 63. In these verses there is a prophetic promise concerning the second destruction of Jerusalem and its temple. Jesus also prophesied this destruction in Luke 19:41-44. This destruction occurred in A.D. 70. Moses is very graphic, describing the conditions during the siege. But if you think this is graphic, you should read the eyewitness account of Josephus, a Jewish historian.

Next is the sixth segment, beginning with verse 64, and following to the end of the chapter. These verses outline the conditions the Jewish people will face during the 2,000 years of their Diaspora (their "scattering" among the nations). There are a number of quality, factual books written concerning the Diaspora of the Jewish people and of the pogroms (the organized extermination of a minority group) that were instituted against them at various times by various nations during that 2,000-year time period. They have suffered greatly as a people. They were blamed for the Bubonic Plague, which was known as the "Black Death." People thought the Jews were poisoning everybody's wells in some sort of plot to kill Christians off so that the Jews could rule the world. The Jewish people were beaten and killed in city after city all over Europe because of this belief.

At other times, the Jews were severely persecuted in Czarist Russia. In England, they were either kicked out of the country, or killed. There was the Spanish Inquisition, and Hitler's Final Solution to the Jewish problem. These pogroms were numerous and widespread. Many of them were instigated by so-called Christians. Christians weren't the only ones, however. The Muslims, from the time of their founder,

Mohammed, did their fair share of killing and persecution as well. Today, anti-Semitism, the hatred and persecution of Jews around the world, is once again sharply on the rise. As Bible-believing Christians who know and understand that the Jews remain God's chosen people, we should speak out in their defense. To not do so would be falling into the same trap that has plagued Christians for centuries.

Deuteronomy 28:64-67 tells us: *"Then the* LORD *will scatter you among all nations, from one end of the earth to the other. There you willl worship other gods, gods of wood and stone which neither you nor your fathers have known. Among those nations you will find no repose, no resting place for the sole of your foot. There the* LORD *will give you an anxious mind, eyes weary with longing, and a despairing heart. You will live in constant suspense, filled with dread both day and night, never sure of your life. In the morning you will say, 'If only it were evening!' and in the evening, 'If only it were morning!' because of the terror that will fill your hearts and the sights that your eyes will see."*

God Promises to Regather

The curse of how the world has treated the Jewish people and divided up their land will come to an end at the end of the Tribulation period. Deuteronomy 30:1-5 gives hope to the Jewish people. It is the light at the end of the tunnel. All of these things have happened to the Jewish people, just as Moses foretold. Therefore, is there any reason not to believe the following verses in Chapter 30 will be true as well? In fact, the promise has already begun to be fulfilled, when Israel became a nation in one day (Isaiah 66:8), in 1948. We are eyewitnesses of this prophetic historic event. Read Deuteronomy 30:1-5: *"When all these blessings and curses I have set before you come upon you and you take them to heart wherever the* LORD *your God disperses you among the nations, and when you and your children return to the* LORD *your God and obey Him with all your heart and with all your soul according to everything I have commanded you today,* **then the LORD your God will restore your fortunes and have compassion on you and gather you again from all the nations where He scattered you.** *Even if you have been banished to the most distant land under the heavens, from there* **the LORD your God will gather you and bring you back**. **He will bring you to the land** *that belonged to your fathers, and you will take possession of it. He will make you more prosperous and numerous than your fathers."* It doesn't matter what part of the Bible you read it from, or what period of time it was written, the message is always the same. The Jewish people will be scattered over the whole earth and they will be reunited again in their ancient homeland at the end of the age.

The Jews Are to Be God's Witnesses

Whether the Jewish people have realized it or not, they have been God's witnesses. Without saying a single word, they have witnessed to the world the truthfulness of Scripture, because of the prophetic promises that have come true concerning them. They have provided overwhelming testimony of the existence and awesomeness of God. There is no other!

The Apostle Paul says in II Corinthians Chapter 3 that a "veil" has covered the minds of the Jewish people. Paul also states in Romans Chapter 9 that he has great sorrow for the Jewish people and would gladly give up his salvation for the sake of his brothers, those of his own race, if that action would give them salvation. He goes on to say in Romans Chapter 11 that the Jews are "enemies" on account of the gospel.

But given all of this, Paul tells us not to be deceived by this falling away. These people are still loved on account of the patriarchs. Paul tells us that *"God's gifts and His call are irrevocable."* (Romans 11:29) All of the prophetic promises made to the patriarchs are irrevocable. The re-establishment of the Jewish people in their homeland today is a result of these irrevocable promises.

Considering all that has happened to the Jewish people throughout their history, and the way they have been scattered throughout the earth, they should not even exist any longer as an identifiable people. They should have been assimilated into the conquering countries and the populations where they were scattered long ago. That they still have their identity as a people, their language, their religion and the purity of their genetic background can only be a result of divine guidance and intervention.

The things that have happened to the Jewish people in the past and the things that are going on in Israel today have always been relevant, are relevant, and will be relevant to both Jews and Christians. No one should be so arrogant as to believe that they, or the "church," have superseded and replaced the irrevocable promises made by God to the Jewish people. This disconnection of Israel from the Scriptures is a dangerous precedent that is being set by many in the Christian church, even in places previously known for their conservative high view of Scripture. God directed that His written Word be written by Jews, to the Jewish people, for their benefit and blessings. Only later were these promises to be **shared** with the Gentiles, i.e., the future Church. However, many within a wide variety of church denominations have invoked a sort of "eminent domain" claim on these blessings and promises, claiming them for themselves and discarding their relevance to Israel, her people and her land. To disconnect the Jewish people and their homeland from the Holy Book that was given to the world through them is a dangerous disservice to the Word of God. You will never prophetically understand the significance of what is going on in Israel and the Middle East if you disconnect Israel from prophecy.

It seems odd that the "Church" has claimed eminent domain on Israel's promised blessings, but not on the promised curses or consequences for not obeying God.

Recapping Isaiah 43:10-11: *"'You are My **witnesses**,' declares the LORD, 'and My **servant whom I have chosen**, so that you may know and believe Me and understand that I am He. Before Me no god was formed, nor will there be one after Me. I, even I, am the LORD, and apart from Me there is no Savior.'"*

These people, the Jews, are God's **witnesses**, and that will never change. They are the servant He has chosen. He will not "unchoose" them! If God went back on any of His promises, that would make Him a liar and a deceiver, and thus untrustworthy. Those attributes would put Him on par with Satan. These are not, and never will be, attributes of God. God is immutable! (Malachi 3:6, Hebrews 13: 8) It is impossible for God to lie. (Hebrews 6:18)

The Fall of Babylon

Isaiah Chapters 44 through 47 speak of the downfall of a future world empire, and the person God would use to bring this about. It

There is No Other God

is the future world empire of Babylon. It was the empire 150 years yet future to Isaiah that would take Jerusalem captive and eventually destroy the city and its temple.

The surviving captives from Israel would be taken to Babylon. The Prophet Jeremiah foretold in Chapters 25 and 29 of his book that this captivity would last for 70 years. At the end of this 70-year period, Babylon would be defeated in a single day and the Israelite captives released to return to their homeland.

Isaiah has this to say in 44:26-28: *"...Who says of Jerusalem, 'It shall be inhabited,' of the towns of Judah, 'They shall be built,' and of their ruins, 'I will restore them,' Who says of Cyrus, 'He is My shepherd and will accomplish all that I please; he will say of Jerusalem, let it be rebuilt, and of the temple, let its foundations be laid.'"* Isaiah continues on about Cyrus in 45:1: *"This is what the LORD says to His anointed, to Cyrus, whose right hand I take hold of to subdue nations before him, to strip kings of their armor, to open doors before him so that gates will not be shut: 'I will go before you and will level the mountains; I will break down gates of bronze and cut through bars of iron.'"* In verse 4: *"For the sake of Jacob My servant, and Israel My chosen, I call you by name and bestow on you a title of honor, though you do not acknowledge Me."*

Even 200 and some years before his birth, God had promised this Cyrus (though unbeknownst to Cyrus personally), that He, God, would open doors before him so that the gates would not be shut. History has recorded when Cyrus, king of the Medo-Persian empire, advanced his army toward Babylon, he first diverted the Euphrates River, causing it to dry up downstream. There were iron gates in the city wall that lowered into the river, so no one could get into and out of the city except through the normal, guarded city gates.

According to the book of Daniel, there was partying and revelry going on in the city that fateful night. Someone "just happened to forget" to put the iron gates down to the riverbed and when the river dried up, Cyrus brought his army in. He took the city and the empire without so much as firing a shot.

So why did God prophetically promise such a small detail as having the gates not shut? And why did He call Cyrus by name? There were Jews living in Babylon and the surrounding countryside. They would have been aware of Isaiah's writings, as well as Jeremiah's prophesied 70 years of captivity. The Prophet Daniel was certainly aware of it, and wrote of it in Chapter 9 of his book. God said He did all this for the sake of Israel, His chosen. When they were eyewitnesses of every fulfilled detail written more than two centuries earlier, then they would know (as Isaiah and Jeremiah had said) that *"I am the* LORD *and there is no other."*

God's Challenge to Us

After God made these prophetic promises in Isaiah 45, and knowing future generations who would be in captivity in Babylon (as well as our present generation) would re-read these passages in Isaiah, He laid down a challenge to them and to us. The challenge is found in 45:20-21: *"Gather together and come; assemble, you fugitives from the nations. Ignorant are those who carry about idols of wood, who pray to gods that cannot save. Declare what is to be, present it—let them take counsel together.* **Who foretold this long ago, and declared it from the distant past?** *Was it not I, the* LORD? *And there is no God apart from me, a righteous God and a Savior; there is none but Me."*

God is throwing down the challenge to these so-called gods and to the people who believe in them. God is saying, in essence: "If you truly are deities as people say you are, then what have you prophesied in the past that has come true, as I have demonstrated? Prophesy future events and their outcomes so that we may see your power and ability." (Compare Isaiah 41:21-22) Elijah threw down the same challenge to the 400-plus prophets of Ba'al in I Kings 18:2-39. Ba'al's power proved to be only imaginary.

There is not one other so-called "holy book" in the world today that has made prophetic promises throughout the centuries that have come to pass. Only the Jewish/Christian Bible, God's Word, has done this, and with 100 percent accuracy. Many say that these other "holy books" are just different ways to the same God. If that were true, then God would be saying the same things in all of them, such as "Love your neighbor as yourself," or "Blessed are the peacemakers." But instead, some of these "holy books" say "Kill the infidel wherever you find them," and "If they do not convert, kill them." These other "holy books" are *not* saying the same thing as God's Word; therefore they do *not* have God as their author. Remember? God is immutable! He is not going to say one thing in the Bible and something else in some other so-called "holy book." <u>We are not worshipping the same God that they are.</u>

Isaiah finishes up in 45:23: *"By Myself I have sworn, My Mouth has uttered in all integrity a word that will not be* **revoked:** *before Me every knee will bow; by Me every tongue will swear."* Paul's letter to the Philippians records the same thing about Jesus in Chapter 2. He states that our *"attitude should be the same as that of Christ Jesus: Who, being in very nature God, did not consider equality with God something to be grasped…"* Then, in verses 10 and 11: *"that at the Name of Jesus every knee should bow, in heaven and on earth and under the earth, and every tongue confess that Jesus Christ is Lord, to the glory of God the Father."* The pre-existing, pre-incarnate Jesus is found throughout the Old Testament, and especially in Isaiah, when you know how to look for Him.

Faith Questions

1. How is Israel a witness to the world?
2. Why was the prophecy concerning Babylon so detailed?
3. How do we know that God isn't speaking through the other so-called "holy books" of the world?

Lesson 19

Isaiah Chapters 46 Through 51
God's Faithfulness to Us

Isaiah Chapter 46 echoes the previous chapter in that God is making very plain the fact that He is the only God. He asks the Israelites (and us, by default) to compare Him with any other known gods. He says: "Look at the evidence." Can any "god" predict the future as He can do, and has done? Have any other "gods" manifested themselves in a miraculous spiritual way, as when the Red Sea was parted, or the column of fire and cloud appeared to lead the Israelites? Isaiah 46:8-10 reads: *"Remember this, fix it in mind, take it to heart, you rebels.* **Remember the former things**, *those of long ago; I am God, and there is no other; I am God, there is none like Me. I make known the end from the beginning, from ancient times, what is still to come. I say: My purpose will stand, and I will do all that I please."*

God is giving the Israelites—and us—one of the keys to faith. He is saying, "Look back in your past and see how many times I have helped you through your troubles." Maybe He was in the middle of your financial difficulty and worked it out to your benefit, and you were surprised. Or maybe He was in the middle of your open heart surgery, which you feared going into, but knew afterward that God had you in the palm of His hand the whole time. When we look back at all the times God has carried us and guided us, even though at the time we perhaps couldn't sense His presence, that should give us trust and faith that He will see us through whatever it is we face.

The other thing God tells us in this verse is that He knows *"the end from the beginning."* After all, He is the "Alpha and Omega, the Beginning and the End, the First and Last." He hasn't missed even one detail of His prophetic promises, as history and archeology have borne out. God is telling us to look back at the fulfilled prophetic promises so we can have confidence looking toward the literal fulfillment of the prophetic promises yet to happen. What is the future God is talking about here in Chapter 46? The future is found in verse 13: *"I am bringing My righteousness near, it is not far away; and My Salvation will not be delayed. I will grant salvation to Zion, My splendor to Israel."* Jesus provided this salvation, and it was right on time, as prophesied by Daniel. We can have this salvation now. It certainly isn't far away. Just say "yes" to Jesus. "Yes, Lord, forgive my sins and come into my heart."

As you continue reading in Isaiah Chapters 47 and 48, notice that God repeats many of the things He has previously said. Whenever God says anything more than once in His written Word, that is an indication that it is very important and we should pay special attention to it. It will be something He does not want us to forget.

In Isaiah 48:14 the use of the word "arm" again comes into play. As previously discussed, the term "arm" is a code word for Jesus. In verse 14b, we read: *"The LORD's chosen ally will carry out His purpose against Babylon; His **Arm** will be against the Babylonians."* Who will be against the Babylonians? If Jesus was against the Babylonians, how could they possibly stand? The truth is, they didn't. Even Moses acknowledged the work and power of Yahweh's Arm in Exodus 15:16. No one, no nation, no spiritual being who comes against or stands against Jesus will themselves be allowed to stand.

Isaiah Chapter 49 is a continuation of the Servant chapters. Verse 1 is a reaffirmation that Jesus was born ("begotten"), not created, and that God has mentioned His name all over the Old Testament, and especially here in Isaiah. Verse 6 is a reaffirmation that Jesus will be a light for the Gentiles, and He will bring salvation to the ends of the earth.

God's Faithfulness to Us

In verse 22, the Sovereign Lord (the compound Name for God) says: *"See, I will beckon to the Gentiles, I will lift up My **Banner** to the peoples…"* God has beckoned to the Gentiles, and many have already seen and acknowledged His living Banner. The main fulfillment of this prophecy follows the time of Israel's restoration, when the Millennial reign of Christ is established. Our studies in Isaiah Chapter 11 indicated that the Banner is the Christ. Christ will be lifted up for all the nations and peoples to see. When Jesus is lifted up this time, it will be to His triumphant glory, not on the cross. When all of this takes place, the last part of verse 26 will be known throughout the earth: *"Then all mankind will know that I, the* (triune) LORD, *am your Savior, your Redeemer, the Mighty One of Jacob."*

The Ransom Price

The next word we want to target in Isaiah's Servant Chapter 50 is the word "ransom." The dictionary defines "ransom" as "the release of a captured person or thing; the price paid for this; to secure release of by payment." We have often heard the phrase: "they are being held for ransom." This is one of the favorite tools of terrorists. Satan has held all of mankind for ransom. Jesus paid the high price of shedding His blood on the cross to secure the release of those being held hostage. Of course, like all terrorists, Satan will be cornered and disarmed, judged and found guilty.

In Isaiah 50:2 God asked Israel a question. *"Was My **Arm** too short to **ransom** you? Do I lack strength to rescue you?"* Here we can clearly see the Arm of God is going to be used for a ransom. Jesus is going to be used for a ransom. Jesus Himself said in Matthew 20:28: *"…just as the Son of Man did not come to be served, but to serve, and to give His life as a **ransom** for many."* This is echoed again in I Timothy Chapter 2 and Hebrews Chapter 9.

How about you? Is the Arm of God too short to rescue, redeem, ransom you? Your ransom has already been paid. Your bail has been made. But you must walk out of the prison you're in, on your own, into the freedom and forgiveness that comes with being born again. "On your own" means you have to make the decision to leave the prison. When you make that decision the Holy Spirit will come alongside to escort you out, to help you and strengthen you.

As this Servant chapter continues, the high ransom price that the "Arm" of God must suffer continues through Chapter 53. We read in 50:5: *"The Sovereign LORD has opened My ears, and I have not been rebellious; I have not drawn back. I offered My back to those who beat Me, My cheeks to those who pulled out My beard; I did not hide My face from mocking and spitting."* Listen to the eyewitness accounts in Matthew 26:67. *"Then they spit in His face and struck Him with their fists. Others slapped Him and said, 'Prophesy to us, Christ. Who hit you?'"* He took this kind of punishment because He loves you.

He wants what is best for you. He wants to live in your heart, to guide and direct your footsteps, so that you may live life to the fullest. This was just one part of the ransom price Jesus had to pay to commute your death sentence.

With what we have learned so far in this study, it should be easy for you to pick out the code words that identify Jesus. In Chapter 51 the "Arm" is used several times, along with the word translated "salvation." The word "salvation" is sometimes translated from different Hebrew words. Some of the Hebrew words translated this way are descriptive of being saved, but have no spiritual implication to them. As discussed at the beginning of this study the Hebrew word, "*yesa*," is the root word for *Yeshua*, which became the Name of Jesus. *Yesa* has spiritual and deistic implications. This word occurs several times in Chapter 51, another Servant chapter, and serves as a good adjunct to identifying Jesus in this chapter. Jesus will stand out in these Servant chapters just as boldly as in any New Testament Scripture.

In Isaiah 51:5-6, it says: *"My righteousness draws near speedily, and My **Salvation** (Jesus) is on the way, and My **Arm** (Jesus) will bring justice to the nations. The islands (nations) will look to Me and wait in hope for My **Arm**. Lift up your eyes to the heavens, look at the earth beneath; the heavens will vanish like smoke, the earth will wear out like a garment and its inhabitants die like flies. But My **Salvation** will last forever, My righteousness will never fail."* Many in the Christian community around the world eagerly wait in hope for the **Arm's** coming for His Church.

The Law (*"Torah"*) was given to the Jewish people at first on stone tablets, then later, on scrolls. This is where the written law was kept. Whenever the Jewish people wanted to know if something was right or wrong, they had to go read and review the law. Jeremiah tells us in 31:33 that it will not always be this way; that after the restoration of all things there will be a different covenant agreement with the Jewish people. *"'This is the covenant I will make with the house of Israel after that time,' declares the LORD. 'I will put My law in their minds and write it on their hearts. I will be their God, and they will be My people.'"* Our job is to love Jewish people, and affirm Jesus to them. The Jewish people gave us the Messiah. Shouldn't we try to lovingly return the favor?

Except for the Messianic Jews, the Jewish people still do not have God's law written on their hearts. But how did the Messianic Jewish believers come to believe in Jesus as their Messiah? All of the first believers in Jesus were Jewish; including all 12 of His disciples and many followers. Then, when the Holy Spirit was given at the Jewish Feast of Weeks (*"Shavuot"* or "Pentecost"), there were 3,000 more Jewish believers added in one day. From then on, the Church grew daily. These and other followers knew the truth about Jesus. But what about today? How did the present-day Messianic Jewish believers come to believe in Yeshua—Jesus—as their Messiah? Somebody had to gently and lovingly show them from Scripture the truth of Jesus. Many of these Jewish believers are taking the saving gospel message to their fellow Jews. As members of the believing Gentile Church, we should financially support and encourage these evangelistic outreaches. We should do it because it is the right thing to do, and it is Biblical.

In Genesis 12:1-3, God told Abraham: *"The LORD had said to Abram, 'Leave your country, your people and your father's household and go to the land I will show you. I will make you into a great nation and I will bless you. I will make your name great, and you will be a blessing.* **I will bless those who bless you, and whoever curses you I will curse***; all the peoples on earth will be blessed through you.'"*

Whoever blesses Abraham and his offspring, God will bless. If you want untold blessings for yourself and your congregation, then you should consider helping your believing Jewish brothers and sisters in their missions, as they share Yeshua with non-believing Jews. Jesus came to the Chosen People first. In Romans 1:16-17, the Apostle Paul stated that the gospel should be taken *"to the Jew first and then to the Gentile."* Again, Paul tells the Roman Gentiles in 15:27: *"They were pleased to do it, and indeed they owe it to them. For if the Gentiles have shared in the Jews' spiritual blessings, they owe it to the Jews to share with them their material blessings."* The Christian community, whether as individuals or as a congregation, should consider some sort of Jewish outreach and share with them our material blessings. Blessings are promised if we do.

These believing Jewish brothers and sisters are just like us. They are saved and they have God's laws written on their hearts. Since the time of Christ and the giving of the Holy Spirit, those who believe in Jesus had and have His law written in their hearts.

With this background, who do you think God is speaking to in Isaiah 50:7? *"Hear Me, you who know what is right, you people who have My law in your **hearts**; do not fear the reproach of men or be terrified by their insults. For the moth will eat them up like a garment; the worm will devour them like wool, but My righteousness will last forever, My **Salvation** through all generations."* He is speaking to us, and to **all** who have ever believed.

The Power of the Arm is Awesome

Isaiah 51:9 continues to have the "Arm" of the LORD as its subject. *"Awake, awake! Clothe yourself with strength, O **Arm** of the LORD; awake, as in days gone by, as in generations of old. Was it not You who cut Rahab to pieces, who pierced that monster through? Was it not You who dried up the sea, the waters of the deep, who made a road in the depths of the sea so that the redeemed might cross over?"* The "Arm" of the LORD was the one who performed these miracles. It was He who did these things, as was pointed out in Lesson 3.

Jude, a half-brother to Jesus, did not believe Jesus was God in the flesh, according to John 7:5. It wasn't until the Resurrection that he came to believe (Acts 1:12-15). Jude verse 5 reveals the pre-incarnate Jesus as being present during the exodus from Egypt: *"Though you already know all this, I want to remind you that the **Lord** delivered His people out of Egypt, but later destroyed those who did not believe."* (In the New Testament, "God" is God, and "Lord" is Jesus.)

I Corinthians 10:1-4 again identifies to us who the Arm was. The Apostle Paul says here that he doesn't want us to be ignorant, misinformed, or allow certain facts to escape us: *"For I do not want you to be ignorant of the fact, brothers, that our forefathers were all under the cloud and that they all passed through the sea. They were all baptized into Moses in the cloud and in the sea. They all ate the same spiritual food and drank the same spiritual drink; for they drank from the spiritual Rock that accompanied them, and that Rock was Christ."*

In Joshua Chapter 4, we have a recounting of how the LORD held back the waters of the Jordan River while the whole nation of Israel crossed into the long-prophesied Promised Land. The stretch of the river that was held back during its flood stage was approximately 15 miles. One of the reasons God did this is recorded in Joshua 4:24. *"He did this so that all the peoples of the earth might know that the **Hand** of the LORD is powerful and so that you might always fear the LORD your God."* The word **hand** in "**Hand** of the LORD" is the same Hebrew word that is translated as "arm" in Isaiah's **Arm** of the LORD. The Hebrew word is *"Yad."* We could just as appropriately say the "**Arm**" of the LORD is powerful" in Joshua 4:24.

There are two assumptions we can make here. First, since the "arm" in "Arm of the LORD" in Isaiah has been shown to be the pre-incarnate Jesus, then it stands to reason that the same Hebrew word translated as "hand" in Joshua could apply as well. Second, the key to this is in the phrase "of the LORD" or "of God." As this study has demonstrated, "Angel of the LORD," "Angel of God," "Glory of the LORD," "Glory of God," "Holy One of God," in fact "anything" "of God," or "of the LORD," is an identifier of the pre-incarnate Jesus. Now when we say anything of God we are referring to descriptions with definite deistic qualities not something subjective like "wrath" of God. Since the Apostle Paul identified Jesus as the "Arm" that parted the Red Sea, we can also see the power of Jesus holding back the Jordan River. Holding back the Jordan River, or parting the Red Sea, feeding the 5,000, raising Lazarus from the dead, and all the other miracles He performed would be absolutely nothing, no effort at all, for the King that created the universe.

Is there anything going on in your life right now that is too great for the King to handle? It may seem like a lot to us, but not to the Holy One of God. With God all things are possible.

You should have absolutely no doubt as to the accuracy and infallibility of God's Word by now. The continuity is just overwhelming. The sameness of message, and the fulfillment of prophecy, is irrefutable evidence to the inerrancy of Scripture.

Faith Questions

1. Why is it important to remember God's leading in your past?
2. What are some of the ways you could reach out to the Jewish people?
3. List some of the things the "Arm of God" was responsible for.

Lesson 20

ISAIAH CHAPTERS 52 AND 53
MANKIND WILL BE WITHOUT EXCUSE

Isaiah Chapter 52 is the last of the gateway Servant chapters leading up to the great Servant chapter, Isaiah 53. We will start by focusing on Isaiah 52:6. *"Therefore My people* (both Christians and Jews) **will** *know My Name; therefore* **in that day** *they will know that it is I who foretold it. Yes, it is I."* Here we harken back to the earlier chapters of Isaiah. **In that day.** In what day? **In that day** when all these prophetic promises come to pass. People will be able to look back at these prophetic fulfillments consummated during their lifetime, and in history, and be without the excuse for not knowing that it was the LORD's doing.

Even in the Apostle Paul's time, he verified to the Romans in Chapter 1:18-20 that *"men are without excuse"* for not believing in God. *"The wrath of God is being revealed from heaven against all the godlessness and wickedness of men who suppress the truth by their wickedness, since what may be known about God is plain to them, because God has made it plain to them. For since the creation of the world God's invisible qualities—His eternal power and divine nature—have been clearly seen, being understood from what has been made, so that* **men are without excuse**.*"* Men are without excuse just by observing the creation around them. How much more will they be without excuse when they see the prophetic promises come true and do nothing about them? John 12:37 tells us: *"Even after Jesus had done all these miraculous signs in their presence, they still would not believe in Him."*

The Apostle Paul quoted Isaiah 52:7 in Romans Chapter 10. In speaking of those who carry the gospel message of salvation, he said *"How beautiful on the mountains are the feet of those who bring good news, who proclaim peace, who bring good tidings, who proclaim salvation, who say to Zion, 'Your God reigns.'"*

Isaiah 52:10 is a profound statement about God, concerning His future action and the revealing of His Son Jesus. God is leading up to a climax here in Isaiah, using graphic descriptive terms, instructing the ancients and us on how we might recognize God's coming to us. (Reference again Luke 19:44.) Isaiah 52:10 reads: *"The LORD will lay bare His **holy Arm** in the sight of all nations, and all the ends of the earth will see the **Salvation** (the Yeshua) of our God."* God is going to lay bare his "Holy Arm."

In ancient times warriors would put hard leather and sometimes iron cladding, or both, on their arms for protection in battle. Without this protection their fighting skills would be greatly jeopardized. When God says He is going to lay bare His holy Arm, He is in effect saying that He is going to make it vulnerable, subject to danger. God could not become any more vulnerable than by becoming flesh and dwelling among us for a while. And that is just what He did.

What the Jewish people, and their priests who supposedly studied the Scriptures, didn't realize was that this verse (and others like it) had a time gap in fulfillment. God laid bare His holy Arm when Jesus came the first time.

However, the ends of the earth did not see Jesus all at once at this time. The ends of the earth will see Jesus, all at the same time, when He comes again at the end of the age. We will see just how bare and vulnerable the Arm of God was, starting in 52:13 and continuing through Chapter 53.

Verse 52:13 reads: [God said] *"See, My servant will act wisely; He will be raised and lifted up and highly exalted."* There are several verses in the Gospels, especially in the book of John, where Jesus refers to being lifted up. Most of them have to do with His ascension into heaven.

In John 8:28, Jesus is referencing being lifted up on the cross. *"So Jesus said, 'When you have lifted up the Son of Man, then you will know that I am the One I claim to be, and that I do nothing on My own but speak just what the Father has taught Me.'"* The disciples knew for sure who He was when He was hanging on the cross. His mother and brothers knew, and His other followers, as well. Even the Roman centurion, standing at the foot of the cross, knew. The high priests knew, as well, but refused to admit it.

Beaten Beyond Recognition

As Isaiah 52:13 makes known, Jesus, the Son of Man, would be lifted up on the cross. What follows in 52:14 is the preview of what Jesus looked like hanging on the cross, 750 years before it happened. *"Just as there were many who were appalled at Him—His appearance was so disfigured beyond that of any man and His form marred beyond human likeness—…"* Jesus was practically unrecognizable hanging on the cross. Yet remember, He could have called 12 legions of angels at any time during the terrible ordeal, to rescue Him. But He did not. Now might be a good time to drop to your knees and tell Him how sorry you are that He had to go through this, and never stop thanking Him that He did.

In John 12:37 (quoted earlier in this lesson), the Apostle John stated that even after all the miraculous signs done in the presence of the Jews, they still did not believe Jesus. John then goes on in verse 38 to quote from Isaiah Chapter 53, which lays this prophecy and identification squarely at the feet of Jesus. *"This was to fulfill the word of Isaiah the prophet: 'LORD, who has believed our message and to whom has the Arm of the LORD been revealed?'"* This, then, becomes the question: To whom has the Arm of the LORD been revealed? Isaiah said that the Arm of the LORD would be revealed. The Apostle John just said that He was revealed to the Jews, and it is most certainly true that they did not recognize Him. Their eyes, ears and hearts had been blinded. As Isaiah stated earlier, Jesus, the Arm of the LORD would be revealed to the whole earth. Has He been revealed to you?

If you've been reading this book, or the Bible, or have observed the creation, then He has been revealed to you. Have you seen Him? II Corinthians 4:4 says: *"The god of this age has blinded the minds of unbelievers, so that they cannot see the light of the gospel of the glory of Christ, who is the image of God."* In II Corinthians 3:14, the Apostle Paul told us that this blinding veil is only taken away by turning to the Lord Jesus.

Jesus has been revealed to the world. He is being revealed, and will continue to be revealed, right up until His visible Second Coming. Isaiah has started to tell us how Jesus, at His first coming, could be recognized physically, and this portrait graphically continues in Isaiah Chapter 53.

By His Wounds We Are Healed

In Isaiah 53:1, we read: *"Who has believed our message and to whom has the **Arm** of the LORD been revealed? He grew up before Him like a tender shoot, and like a root out of dry ground. He had no beauty or majesty to attract us to Him, **nothing in His appearance that we should desire Him**."* Isaiah said when Jesus comes that His appearance would hold no physical attraction for us. Unlike Moses, whom the Jewish historian Josephus reputes to be a beautiful child and handsome man, Jesus, in contrast, would be homely. We will not be attracted to Him by His physical prowess or appearance. Our movie stars, many of our professional athletes, and others have this attractiveness about them, but not Jesus.

We have just considered the physical beauty of Jesus, or rather the lack of it, but what about His majesty? Majesty, and the trappings of it, can make even a homely person attractive, in a worldly way. Isaiah said Jesus would have none of that, either. He did not come the first time as a king or somebody glamorous; He came as a lowly servant. Some of the paintings of Jesus are very beautiful, no doubt reflecting the love of the artist for his Lord, but these do not reflect the physical image that Isaiah portrays.

If we are going to be attracted to Jesus it can't be based on worldly standards. It has to be based on Godly, Biblical standards. His goodness, His representation of ultimate Truth, His miracles, His bringing people back from death to life, enable us to recognize Him from the physical and spiritual descriptions given to us through Isaiah and others. He is God, who dwelt among us, and there is no other.

Isaiah continues in verse 53:3: *"He was **despised and rejected by men**, a man of sorrows, and familiar with suffering. Like one from whom* men hide their faces He was despised, and we esteemed Him not." He was despised and rejected by **you**. There are many, many people out there who despise and reject Jesus just like you. Some, like you, repent and ask Jesus for forgiveness; others despise and reject Him to their dying days. The point is, we have all despised and rejected Jesus at some time in our lives.

Verse 53:4 reads: *"Surely He took up our infirmities and carried our sorrows, yet we considered Him stricken by God, smitten by Him, and afflicted."* Isaiah writes in the past and present tense as though he were standing at the foot of the cross. Of those standing at the foot of the cross, many were believers, and except for the believing Roman centurion, they were Jewish believers. And they all stood there wondering why God would allow such humiliation, such physical pain and agony, such an injustice in taking the life of an innocent man. All Jesus ever did was talk about His Heavenly Father, and healed the infirmities of the down and out. Yes, He did—and does—take up our infirmities and carry our sorrows.

Matthew 8:14-17 tells us: *"When Jesus came into Peter's house, He saw Peter's mother-in-law lying in bed with a fever. He touched her hand and the fever left her, and she got up and began to wait on Him. When evening came, many who were demon-possessed were brought to Him, and He drove out the spirits with a word and healed all the sick. This was to fulfill what was spoken through the prophet Isaiah: 'He took up our infirmities and carried our diseases.'"*

Even today, we wonder why Godly people suffer. According to the faith chapter, Hebrews 11, many distinguished people of old were allowed to do great and marvelous things based on their faith. But others, because of their faith, were tortured, faced jeers and flogging, chained and put in prison; they were stoned, sawed in two, put to death by sword. They were destitute, persecuted and mistreated. The world was not worthy of them. These were all commended for their faith. But most people considered these "suffering servants" stricken by God and smitten by Him, which could not be further from the truth. However, then, as now, God does not often answer our "why" questions. In Malachi 3:13-18, God does promise us that there is a time coming when we will again see the distinction between those who serve God and those who do not.

Returning to Isaiah 53:4, we read: *"But He was **pierced** for our transgressions, He was crushed for our iniquities; the punishment that brought us peace was upon Him, and by His wounds we are healed."* This piercing of the hands and feet by hanging a person on the cross was a uniquely Roman form of capital punishment, dealt out to non-Roman citizens. When Isaiah scripted this prophetic promise, the city of Rome was just being founded.

In Psalm 22, with Jesus speaking in the first person, it says: *"They have pierced My hands and My feet."* Jesus also gave us intimate details of His suffering in this Psalm. Verses 7 and 8 indicate mental humiliation: *"All who see Me mock Me; they hurl insults, shaking their heads: 'He trusts in the* LORD*; let the* LORD *rescue Him. Let Him deliver Him, since He delights in Him.'"* Verses 14 and 15 graphically reveal His physical agony and pain. *"I am poured out like water, and all My bones are out of joint. My Heart has turned to wax; it has melted away within Me. My strength is dried up like a potsherd, and My tongue sticks to the roof of My mouth; you lay Me in the dust of death"* Verses 16 through 18 detail the callousness of the perpetrators: *"Dogs have surrounded Me; a band of evil men has encircled Me, they have pierced My hands and My feet. I can count all My bones; people stare and gloat over Me. They divide My garments among them and cast lots for My clothing."*

These visions of the suffering Christ were given to King David 1,000 years preceding the event. That kind of detailed accuracy is duplicated in no other so-called "holy book" in the world today. That kind of accuracy can only have God as its source.

Do you want to make Isaiah 53:4 personal? Then repeat out loud: "He was pierced for **my** transgressions, He was crushed for **my** iniquities; the punishment that brought **me** peace was upon Him, and by His wounds **I am healed**." The Apostle Peter made no bones concerning who Isaiah was writing about in I Peter 2:24: *"He Himself bore our sins in His body on the tree, so that we might die to sins and live for righteousness;* ***by His wounds you have been healed****."*

Continuing in Isaiah 53 with verses 6 and 7: *"We all, like sheep, have gone astray, each of us has turned to his own way; and the Lord laid on Him*

Mankind Will Be Without Excuse

the iniquity of us all. He was oppressed and afflicted, yet He did not open His mouth; He was led like a lamb to the slaughter, as a sheep before her shearers is silent, so He did not open His mouth." This prophecy has been borne out by the eyewitness account recorded in Matthew 27:11-14: *"Meanwhile Jesus stood before the governor, and the governor asked Him, 'Are you the King of the Jews?' 'Yes, it is as you say,' Jesus replied. When He was accused by the chief priests and the elders,* **He gave no answer***. Then Pilate asked Him, 'Don't you hear how many things they are accusing you of?'* **But Jesus made no reply***, not even to a single charge, to the great amazement of the governor."*

Isaiah 53:8a reads: *"By oppression and judgment He was taken away."* The Gospels record His arrest by the high priest and the temple guards. He was judged and found innocent by Pilate, but sentenced to death and was taken away due to political pressure. Verse 8 then continues: *"And who can speak of His descendants? For He was cut off from the land of the living; for the transgressions of my people He was stricken."* Isaiah posed this question knowing full well that the Savior would not be married, nor would He have children. Anyone who tries to tell us differently is a liar and a deceiver, and the truth is not in him. The background theme of these verses is always the same. It is because of our transgressions and sins against the Almighty God that Jesus must suffer these things.

Going on with verse 9: *"He was assigned a grave with the* **wicked***, and with the* **rich** *in His death, though He had done no violence, nor was any deceit found in His mouth."* In His death on the cross, Jesus hung there with two thieves; one on His left and one on His right. They were most certainly wicked men. One of these wicked men repented, just in time. Then there were the insults hurled at Him by the priestly class as they passed by.

These examples are fairly inclusive of the wicked men unlawfully murdering Jesus. But what of the rich? John 19:38-39 tells us: *"Later, Joseph of Arimathea asked Pilate for the body of Jesus. Now Joseph was a disciple of Jesus, but secretly because he feared the Jews. With Pilate's permission, he came and took the body. He was accompanied by Nicodemus, the man who earlier had visited Jesus at night. Nicodemus brought a mixture of myrrh and aloes, about 75 pounds."* Both of these men, Joseph and Nicodemus, were rich men. Joseph had to be wealthy to be able to afford a tomb chiseled out of the side of a mountain. That was a very labor-intensive job. At least two large-size rooms were carved out of solid rock. Only the rich could afford these types of graves. And Nicodemus? He was a Pharisee. In order to be a Pharisee, one had to be highly-educated and be able to trace his lineage back to King David. Then, just as now, education was not cheap. One had to be from a wealthy family in order to qualify for becoming a Pharisee. Both men were members of the exclusive, 71-member ruling body known as the Sanhedrin. Because of Joseph's wealth and political position within the Sanhedrin, he would have been allowed to seek, and receive, audience with Pilate. For Pilate to grant this favor, this gesture of reconciliation to Joseph of Arimathea, would be an attempt at political placating.

Here again, Isaiah has the prophetic promise concerning the rich nailed. Just consider Joseph having a freshly-cut, unused tomb, and Nicodemus having 75 pounds of spices that he could not have purchased on short notice due to it being a holiday weekend. After all, it was Passover. This begs the question: Did they know Jesus would be crucified ahead of time? They had to know ahead of time in order to have these things prepared as they did. As far as Joseph is concerned, he might have known months ahead of time, considering the labor-intensive job that had to be performed in preparing the tomb. The evidence indicates that they knew. These two men were not asked to give up their wealth to be followers of Jesus, like the rich young ruler was. However, they certainly put everything they owned and stood for at risk, by exposing themselves to the imminent dangers inherent with being associated with Jesus in any way.

Sometimes we are not all asked to give up everything to follow Jesus, only that we be willing to sacrifice everything, if necessary. Are you willing? There is no doubt Joseph and Nicodemus were believers, even if they were "secret service" believers. The twelve disciples didn't have a clue that this was going to happen to Jesus, even though He had told them. These two were different. God was, no doubt, encouraging these two men to do what they did. It is possible that they didn't know or realize what they were doing would fulfill prophecy, but they believed Jesus when He told them that He must be lifted up, referring to His death on the cross.

In Isaiah 53:11 we read: *"After the suffering of His soul, He will see the light of life, and be satisfied; by His knowledge My righteous Servant will **justify many**, and He will bear their iniquities."* "Righteous Servant" now becomes a name, or title, that we can identify with the Lord Jesus. He will justify many. Acts 13:38-39 tells us: *"Therefore, my brothers, I want you to know that through Jesus the forgiveness of sins is proclaimed to you. Through Him everyone who believes is **justified** from everything you could not be justified from by the law of Moses."* The "justification of many" is limited to those who believe.

When you come to believe and confess, you have crossed over from death unto life. (John 5:24) What is God's will concerning mankind? I Timothy 2:4 and II Peter 3:9 state that God wants all men to be saved and to come to a knowledge of the truth. Is that what God wants? Yes! Will that happen? No! The reality is, only the many who believe will be **justified.**

Jesus to the Rescue

Continuing with Isaiah 53:12: *"Therefore, I will give Him a portion among the great; He will divide the spoils with the strong, because He poured out His life unto death, and was numbered with the transgressors. For He bore the sin of many and made **intercession** for the transgressors."*

He made "intercession for transgressors." What does this mean? The act of interceding is the act of taking our part, of defending us. So who is Jesus going to defend the transgressors from? Romans 8:34 says Christ Jesus is at the right hand of God and is also interceding for us. So is Jesus defending us from God's accusations? There are a number of Scriptures that indicate who Jesus is defending us from. One such Scripture comes from Zechariah 3:1-4. In this passage, Jesus is identified as the "Angel of the LORD." Only Jesus has the ability to take away your sin, which is what this "Angel of the LORD" does. Verse 1 says: *"Then he showed me Joshua* (not the Joshua that led the Israelites) *the high priest standing before the Angel of the LORD, and **Satan** standing at his right side to **accuse** him."* Verses 3 and 4 continue: *"Now Joshua was dressed in filthy clothes as he stood before the Angel.* (Filthy clothes are a representation of sin. Compare Isaiah 64:6.) *The Angel said to those who were standing before Him, 'Take off his filthy clothes.' Then He said to Joshua, 'See, I have* *taken away your sin, and I will put rich garments on you.'"* Zechariah goes on to say these things are symbolic of things to come. In Revelation Chapter 12, verses 9 and 10 say it is Satan who leads the whole world astray, and he is *"the accuser of our brothers, who accuses them before our God day and night…"*

It is Satan who accuses us. It is Jesus who intercedes for us. It is Jesus who stands there, answering each and every accusation that Satan hurls at us. Jesus stands there, and He can point to His thorn-crowned head, His severely torn body from the Roman cat-o-nine tails, the beatings and the plucking out of His beard, His nail-pierced hands and feet—and most of all—He can point to His shed blood. He can stand there and say to His Father, "He is mine. I paid the price, I paid the ransom. He believes in me, I love him, and I want him to be with Me forever."

Oh, what a price He paid! We all have filthy clothes on as we stand before the throne of God. Do you want Jesus to say "Well done, good and faithful servant?" Or do you want Him to say, "I know you not; depart from Me, you doer of iniquity?" It is up to you.

Isaiah saw Jesus' glory "in detail" and wrote about Him!

Considering all that is written about Jesus, His ministry, His death, burial, and resurrection, in Isaiah as well as the other prophets and authors of the Old Testament, we are able to say, <u>with all respect for God's entire Word</u>: "There is nothing new in the New Testament."

There once was a story about a king. He was a good king. He cared for his subjects' well-being. His subjects loved and adored him. Everyone got along in his kingdom. One day, there was a report given to the king that somebody had reported a theft. Now, there was a law in the kingdom that said anyone caught stealing would receive 39 lashes with a whip. A few days later the king's servant came to him and said, "We have found the thief." "Bring him to me," said the king. "But Sir," said the servant, "the thief is your mother!"

Now what was the king going to do? He loved his mother and couldn't bear to see her whipped. But what about those in the rest of the kingdom? Wouldn't they say, "The law applies to everyone except the king and his family?" Wouldn't they think, "If it is okay for the king's mother to do this, it ought to be okay for us, as well?" The king pondered these things in his heart. Then he decided that his mother should receive the punishment. So he set the day for her punishment. On that day she was brought into the king's presence, and tied to a stake. The servant with the whip was in place. Then the king arose from his throne, took off his robe and removed his shirt, walked over to his mother, stood behind her and wrapped his arms around her. Then he said, "Let the punishment begin." The king took the punishment instead of his mother; the law was satisfied, the price was paid.

This is exactly what Jesus does for us who believe and confess His holy Name. He took the punishment that we deserved, because He loves us so much.

No Reason to Doubt the Promises

With the many prophetic promises we have examined in this study thus far, and considering their literal fulfillment in every detail, is there any reason to doubt the prophecies yet future to us will be fulfilled in any other way but literally? How many pages of prophetic promises concerning Israel's re-establishment in the land, and the events significant to prophetic fulfillment, do we need to tear out here in Isaiah (or in the whole Bible, for that matter) in order to make replacement theology work? That is what would be required; to either ignore those promises, or change their literal meaning.

Ignoring and/or changing literal meaning in Scripture is occurring much too often within the "church" today. This is not to call anyone's salvation into question; only to suggest possibly revisiting this issue if you do subscribe to replacement theology.

Scripture has already set the precedent concerning literal fulfillment; it will not deviate from this already-established course. Everyone, from the simplest cognitive mind to the most educated, will be able to literally see, understand and recognize the literal future fulfillment of prophetic Scripture.

Faith Questions

1. Why will mankind be without excuse concerning knowing God?
2. How will Jesus' Second Coming differ from His First Coming?
3. Why is the Isaiah 53 account so important to Bible "believability?"

Lesson 21

ISAIAH CHAPTERS 54 THROUGH 66
COME TO THE WATERS

Chapter 53 is definitely the high point in the book of Isaiah. The chapters that follow are somewhat anti-climactic, but no less important.

Isaiah 54:11-12 gives us a picture of the new Jerusalem. *"Oh afflicted city, lashed by storms and not comforted, I will build you with stones of turquoise, your foundations with sapphires. I will make your battlements of rubies, your gates of sparkling jewels, and all your walls of precious stones."* Revelation Chapter 21 will give you a more detailed look at the city that comes down from heaven as a gift from God. The visions God gave His prophets, even though they are over 1200 years apart, were always the same. The number of details can vary, but not the main focus or content of the vision.

Isaiah 55:1-2 bids us: *"Come, all you who are thirsty, come to the **waters**; and you who have no money, buy and eat! Come, buy wine and milk without money and without cost. Why spend money on what is not bread, and your labor on what does not satisfy? Listen, listen to Me, and eat what is good, and your soul will delight in the richest of fare."* If you thirst, "come to the waters." What waters? How can you come, if you don't know what they are or where to look for them? Here again, if we let Scripture interpret Scripture we will be able to answer this question.

Let's return to Revelation Chapter 21. This time we look at verse 6. *"He said to me: 'It is done. I am the Alpha and the Omega, the Beginning and the End. To him who is thirsty, I will give drink without cost from the spring of the Water of Life.'"* Going on to Revelation 22:17, we read: *"The Spirit and the bride say, 'Come!' And let him who hears say, 'Come!' Whoever is thirsty, let him come; and whoever wishes, let him take the free gift of the Water of Life."*

What do we know about the "Water" from the Scriptures thus far? There is an invitation to come to it. It is our choice to come or not come. If we do come to the Water, it has no cost. It is a free gift. Now we also know that the water is the "Water of Life." But we still don't know where the Water comes from and how to get it. The remaining answers can be found in John 7:37-39: *"On the last and greatest day of the Feast, Jesus stood and said in a loud voice, 'If anyone is **thirsty**, let him come to Me and **drink**. Whoever **believes** in Me, as the Scripture has said, streams of **Living Water** will flow from within him.' By this He meant the **Spirit**, whom those who believe in Him were later to receive. Up to that time the Spirit had not been given, since Jesus had not yet been glorified."* Just like Jesus told the woman at the well: whoever drinks from the Water He gives would never thirst again.

The **Living Water** that comes from Jesus, and is given to those who believe in Him, is the Holy Spirit. It flows through Jesus to us. It flows through us and out of us to others and gives glory back to Jesus. If we do our part and allow the Holy Spirit to work through us, the circle will be unbroken. So when Isaiah says in 55:1 *"Come, all you who are thirsty, come to the waters,"* now we know just exactly what he means: come to the Holy Spirit of God and feast on the richest of fare.

Isaiah continues on in verses 7-8: *"Let the wicked forsake his way and the evil man his thoughts. Let him turn to the LORD, and He will have mercy on him, and to our God, for He will freely pardon. 'For your thoughts are not My thoughts; neither are your ways My ways,' declares the LORD. 'As the heavens are higher than the earth, so are My ways higher than your ways and My thoughts than your thoughts.'"* We just need to take heed, and not think more highly of ourselves than we should.

God's Word Will Accomplish His Desires

In verses 10 and 11, God gives Isaiah an insight into the earth's water cycle. Science didn't confirm this until recent centuries. *"As the rain and snow come down from heaven and do not return to it without watering the earth and making it bud and flourish, so that it yields seed for the sower and bread for the eater, so is My Word that goes out from My mouth. It will not return to Me empty, but will accomplish what I desire and achieve the purpose for which I send it."*

When God speaks about His Word going out from His mouth and not returning to Him empty, do we subconsciously put a time limit on this action? When we speak God's Word to someone, and as a result that person comes to Christ, is that the end of the story? Is God's Word returning to Him, accomp-lishing that which He desired? Consider this: what if that person told their children, and then their grandchildren, for generations to come? Could not their salvation be traced back to you being obedient to speak and release God's Word and power for salvation? Once we speak and release God's Word into the world, we ultimately do not know how far around the world, how far into the future or how many people it will affect, as His Word goes forth. Only God knows. You will, however, find out when you meet them in heaven. Will that be our heavenly reward when we look around us and see the possible multitudes there in heaven because of our faithfulness to share God's Word? Even if the result was only one person there would be great rejoicing in heaven. (Luke 15:7). This is, after all, part of the prayer Jesus offered in John 17:20: *"My prayer is not for them (apostles) alone.* ***I pray also for those who will believe in me through their message.****"*

Some of those in the future will be able to trace their salvation through us. But all of us will trace our salvation through the apostles who received it from Jesus. Jesus spoke only what the Father told Him. Thus, God the Father's Word will return to Him, accomplishing that which He has desired and the purpose for which He sent it.

Isaiah Chapter 56 starts out by encouraging us to *"Maintain justice and do what is right, for My* **Salvation** (Yeshua) *is close at hand and My righteousness will soon be revealed."* Earlier in Isaiah's writings, God warned the Israelites of their impending doom due to their failure to maintain justice, their failure to do what was right and their failure to honor and worship God in a worthy manner. Isaiah continues this theme in Chapter 56, exhorting the Israelites and the foreigners who bind themselves to the LORD to serve Him, to seek and maintain justice, and to do what is right.

Isaiah 57:1-2 poses somewhat of an answer to the "why" question that accompanies what we would consider the premature death of God-fearing people. *"The righteous perish, and no one ponders it in his heart; devout men are taken away, and no one understands that the righteous are taken away to be spared from evil. Those who walk uprightly enter into peace; they find rest as they lie in death."* There can be times in peoples' lives when tragedy has struck the family. There are all sorts of scenarios that could be developed here. No matter what the scenario, the emotion stays the same. Comments can go something like this: "I'm glad mother wasn't around to see this. It would have broken her heart." Or, "Grandpa would roll over in his grave if he knew about this." The idea is that God, in His mercy, sometimes spares His children from future heartbreaking grief, through what seems to us like "premature" death.

Maybe you have witnessed this, as well: two people who have been married for a long time, one spouse a committed believer and the other a "hereditary" Christian ("hereditary" Christian being someone who was born into the Christian faith, who claims to be Christian, but has no evidence in their life to support that claim). The believing spouse, who has been unable to effect change in the unbelieving spouse, experiences a somewhat premature death. The family wonders why the Lord would take this godly, giving person instead of the other one. But down the road, the surviving spouse remarries, and through that union comes to know the Lord in a saving way. Then we begin to see the hand of God at work and perhaps begin to understand "why." God is sovereign. His ways are higher than our ways, and His thoughts are higher than our thoughts.

The Kind of Fasting God Desires

In Isaiah Chapter 58, God has some very strong issues with the Israelite people, and with us as well. The issue has to do with fasting and its proper use and meaning. God starts out in Isaiah 58 telling the Israelites what is wrong with the way they are fasting, and their attitude toward fasting. Then He instructs them in the kind of fasting that He chooses. Starting in verse 3, we read: *"'Why have we fasted,' they say, 'and you have not seen it? Why have we humbled ourselves, and you have not noticed?' 'Yet on the day of your fasting, you do as you please and exploit all your workers. Your fasting ends in quarreling and strife, and in striking each other with wicked fists. You cannot fast as you do today and expect your voice to be heard on high. Is this the kind of fast I have chosen, only a day for a man to humble himself? Is it only for bowing one's head like a reed and for lying on sackcloth and ashes? Is that what you call a fast, a day acceptable to the* LORD*? Is this not the kind of fasting I have chosen: to loose the chains of injustice and untie the cords of the yoke, to set the oppressed free and break every yoke? Is it not to share your food with the hungry and to provide the poor wanderer with shelter—when you see the naked, to clothe him, and not turn away from your own flesh and blood?'"*

God was not accepting their ritual of fasting, just the same as He did not accept their worship and prayers recorded in Isaiah Chapter 1. They were doing it wrong, and for the wrong reasons. What about us? Do we fast for the wrong reasons? Are there other things God would prefer us to do in the name of a fast? Loosening the chains of injustice, setting the oppressed free, feeding the poor and clothing the naked? Jesus told us in Matthew 25:34-40: *"Then the King will say to those on His right, 'Come, you who are blessed by My Father, take your inheritance, the kingdom prepared for you since the creation of the world. For I was hungry and you gave Me something to eat, I was thirsty and you gave Me something to drink, I was a stranger and you invited Me in, I needed clothes and you clothed Me, I was sick and you looked after Me, I was in prison and you came to visit Me.' Then the righteous will answer Him, 'Lord, when did we see You hungry and feed You, or thirsty and give You something to drink? When did we see You a stranger and invite You in, or needing clothes and clothed You? When did we see You sick or in prison and go to visit You?' The King will reply, 'I tell you the truth, whatever you did for one of the least of these brothers of Mine, you did for Me.'"*

God Does Not Change

God has not changed His message. It just seems that way in the Old Testament because of the spiritual malpractice perpetrated by the Jewish people. Because the priests were not teaching, preaching, and exhorting their followers to truth, righteousness and godly living, they were guilty of spiritual malpractice. Doctors can harm—and even cause the death of their patients—through negligence or ignorance, and be guilty of medical malpractice. So also harm and spiritual death can be done to those who are babes in the faith. How many pastors and seminary professors today, and even Sunday School teachers, are guilty of spiritual malpractice by not teaching directly and correctly from the Word of God? Has a veil has covered their eyes? Only through Christ is it taken away.

Isaiah Chapter 59 again speaks of the "Arm of the LORD" in two different places. The question asked in Isaiah 50:2b, *"Was My Arm too short to ransom you?"* is answered here in 59:1: *"Surely the Arm of the LORD is not too short to save, nor His ear too dull to hear.* **But your iniquities have separated you from your God**; *your sins have hidden His face from you, so that He will not hear."* Jesus is more than capable of saving us. But if we continue in unrepentant sin, then His hands are tied. God never sends anybody to Hell; by our own actions (or inactions) we send ourselves there. By our own failure to repent of our sins and acknowledge Jesus as Lord and Savior, we, by our own choice, send ourselves to Hell. As the verse says, we have separated ourselves from God.

God was very displeased that there was so much sin and corruption in the human race, and particularly in His chosen Jewish people. There was no one among the population who could atone for sin on a permanent basis. No one was qualified by living a perfect, sin-free life. In Isaiah 59:16 we read: *"He saw that there was no one, He was appalled that there was no one to intervene; so His own* **Arm** *worked salvation for Him, and His own righteousness sustained Him."*

Verse 17 tells us: *"He put on righteousness as His breastplate, and the helmet of salvation on His head…."* The "breastplate of righteousness" and the "helmet of salvation" were some of the things that Jesus girded Himself with. Salvation and righteousness are the things that Jesus gives to those who believe in Him. The Apostle Paul instructed the Ephesians to claim these free gifts so that they – and we – can stand firm against the devil's schemes. Ephesians 6:14-18 says: *"Stand firm then, with the belt of truth buckled around your waist, with the* **breastplate of righteousness** *in place, and with your feet fitted with the readiness that comes from the gospel* *of peace. In addition to all this, take up the shield of faith, with which you can extinguish all the flaming arrows of the evil one. Take the **helmet of salvation** and the sword of the Spirit, which is the Word of God. And pray in the Spirit on all occasions with all kinds of prayers and requests. With this in mind, be alert and always keep on praying for all the saints."*

Isaiah Chapter 60 highlights how Israel will be honored by the nations during the Millennial reign of Christ. We will emphasize the first and last verses. Verse 1 reads: *"Arise, shine, for your Light has come, and the **Glory of the LORD** rises upon you."* That is a prophetic promise. In verse 22:b, we read: *"I am the LORD; in its time I will do this swiftly."*—another promise.

Before we start Chapter 61 of Isaiah, a little background Scripture is in order. Reading from Luke 4:16-22: *"Jesus went to Nazareth, where He had been brought up, and on the Sabbath Day He went into the synagogue, as was His custom. And He stood up to read. The scroll of the Prophet Isaiah was handed to Him. Unrolling it, He found the place where it is written: 'The Spirit of the Lord is on Me, because He has anointed Me to preach good news to the poor. He has sent Me to proclaim freedom for the prisoners and recovery of sight for the blind, to release the oppressed, and to proclaim the year of the Lord's favor.' Then He rolled up the scroll, gave it back to the attendant and sat down. The **eyes** of everyone in the synagogue were **fastened** on Him, and He began saying to them, 'Today this scripture is fulfilled in your hearing.'"*

Why were everyone's eyes fastened on Jesus? There could be several answers given here, but one that is obvious was that Jesus did not complete the reading. He stopped in mid-verse. So why did He stop in mid-verse? Because, as He told the people, this much of Isaiah's prophecy had now been fulfilled in their hearing. For someone to say this part of the prophecy has been fulfilled would cause His listeners to gasp. No one ever talked to them that way before. And yet, they became furious at Jesus' explanation. Jesus read the first two and one-half verses of Isaiah Chapter 61, and then stopped. Because of His arrival on earth and the beginning of His ministry at age 30, that part had been fulfilled. The rest of Chapter 61 will not be fulfilled until the Millennial reign of Christ.

As a side note, why did Jesus wait until He was 30 years old to begin His ministry? He certainly would have been mature enough at age

20, or probably any age for that matter. Under the Rabbinic laws, one could not become a priest until He reached age 30. In order to fulfill the law, Jesus didn't start His earthly ministry until He was old enough to fill that priestly role, and become our great High Priest in the *"order of Melchizedek."* (Psalm 110:4, Hebrews 5:5-6)

Isaiah Chapter 62 uses the word "Arm" in reference to Jesus. Isaiah Chapter 63 uses the word "Arm" and repeats what he says in chapter 59. Isaiah 63:9 gives us a new code word for Jesus: *"In all their distress He too was distressed, and the **Angel of His Presence saved** them."* The word "saved" used here is from the root word *"yesa"* or *"Yeshua."* The Hebrew word translated as "presence" does not shed any light in identifying God the Father. But who else's presence could it be? The phrase "Angel of His Presence" has action. The action is that it **saved** them. "Saved" and "salvation" both come from the same root word, "Yeshua." *Yeshua* (Jesus) is the only One who can save! Therefore, the "Angel of His Presence" must be Jesus.

Isaiah Chapter 64:4 tells us: *"Since ancient times no one has heard, no ear has perceived, no eye has seen any God beside You, who acts on behalf of those who **wait** for Him."* God acts on behalf of those who wait for Him. Is there anyone else you would rather have acting for you on your behalf? It is another promise.

The Lord's Timing

Waiting on the Lord is an important spiritual concept. The Apostle Paul gave the Corinthians (and us) some of the benefits for waiting on the Lord. We read in I Corinthians 1:7-8: *"Therefore you do not lack any spiritual gift as you eagerly **wait** for our Lord Jesus Christ to be revealed. He will keep you strong to the end, so that you will be blameless on the day of our Lord Jesus Christ."* Now, that is acting on your behalf!

Waiting also implies something else: patience. Is there something going on in your life where you have taken it to the Lord in prayer, and it has been a while? Have patience, wait on the Lord. His timing is perfect. The Bible has many examples where believing people didn't wait on the Lord's timing. Abraham and Sarah come to mind, thinking they needed to take matters into their own hands in order for Abraham to have a son. Or, there was Jonah, running away from God. By not waiting on the Lord, they caused a lot of grief for themselves, and so can we.

There is another parallel to Isaiah 64:4 in I Corinthians 2:9-10: *"However, as it is written: 'No eye has seen, no ear has heard, no mind has conceived what God has prepared for those who love Him,' but God has revealed it to us by His Spirit."*

Thus far in our study of Isaiah, God's main message has been toward His chosen Jewish people. He has allowed us, non-Jewish people – Gentiles – to be privy to His teachings, His writings, and even to be the recipients of His promises. He demonstrates this in the first verse of Isaiah Chapter 65. *"I revealed myself to those who did not ask for Me; I was found by those who did not seek Me. To a nation that did not call on My Name, I said, 'Here am I, here am I.'"* That is us. As non-Jewish people who believe, we have been grafted in to the branches (Romans 11:16-21).

The New Heaven and Earth

For all of us believing "branches," whether natural or grafted in, that are supplied by the Root (Jesus), Chapter 65 holds a new promise for us. That promise is a new Heaven and a new Earth. This promise in Isaiah 65 has parallels in Isaiah Chapter 11 and Revelation Chapter 21.

As we read starting in 65:17 to the end of the chapter, we will find that there are conditions that are ascribed to the Millennial reign of Christ, and there are conditions that will be in place when the new Heaven and the new Earth are created. Isaiah talks about death and dying that will occur on a very limited basis during the Millennial reign of Christ. No such condition will occur in the new Heaven and Earth.

Beginning in verse 17 and continuing through verse 25, Isaiah tells us what the LORD says: *"Behold, I will create new heavens and a new earth. The former things will not be remembered, nor will they come to mind. But be glad and rejoice forever in what I will create, for I will create Jerusalem to be a delight and its people a joy. I will rejoice over Jerusalem and take delight in my people; the sound of weeping and crying will be heard in it no more. Never again will there be in it an infant that lives but a few days, or an old man that does not live out his years; he who dies at a hundred would be thought a mere youth; he who fails to reach a hundred would be considered accursed. They will build houses and dwell in them; they will plant vineyards and eat their fruit. No longer will they build houses and others live in them, or plant and others eat. For as the days of a tree, so will be the days of My people; My chosen ones will long enjoy the works of their hands. They will not toil in vain or bear children doomed to misfortune; for they will be people blessed by the* LORD, *they and their descendants with them. Before they call I will answer; while they are still speaking I will hear. The wolf and the lamb will feed together, and the lion will eat straw like the ox, but dust will be the serpent's food. They will neither harm nor destroy in all My holy mountain,' declares the* LORD.*"* We should yearn for that day like we have never yearned before.

In Chapter 66, God gives us a little insight into His awesomeness, and what He expects from us. Verses 1 and 2 tell us: *"This is what the* LORD *says: 'Heaven is My throne and the earth is My footstool. Where is the house you will build for Me? Where will My resting place be? Has not My* **Hand** *(Arm) made all these things, and so they came into being?' declares the* LORD. **'This is the one I esteem: he who is humble and contrite in spirit, and trembles at My Word.'"**

> *"In the beginning was the* **Word***, and the* **Word** *was with God, and the* **Word was God***. He was with God in the beginning. Through Him all things were made; without Him nothing was made that has been made. In Him was life, and that life was the* **Light** *of men. The* **Light** *shines in the darkness, but the darkness has not understood it. There came a man who was sent from God; his name was John. He came as a witness to testify concerning that* **Light***; he came only as a witness to the* **Light***. The true* **Light** *that gives light to every man was coming into the world. He was in the world, and though the world was made through Him,* **the world did not recognize Him***. He came to that which was His own, but His own did not receive Him. Yet to all who received Him, to those who believed in His Name,* **He gave the right to become children of God***—children born not of natural descent, nor of human*

*decision or a husband's will, but **born of God**. **The Word became flesh** and lived for a while among us. We have seen His **Glory**, the **Glory** of the one and only Son, who came from the Father, full of grace and truth."* (John 1:1-14)

Lord, may these teachings always remain in their hearts. Amen.

Faith Questions

1. What is the "Living Water," and where does it come from?
2. Why speak to someone about Jesus?
3. Why will God's Word not return to Him empty?
4. Are your fasts pleasing to God?
5. What separates us from God?
6. How can we help protect ourselves against Satan's arrows?
7. Why did Jesus wait until He was 30 years old to officially start His ministry?

NAMES AND TITLES OF JESUS

Here are the names and titles Isaiah uses to identify Jesus in his writings, including cross-references from other books of the Bible referred to in this study.

And He will be called:
The Glory of the LORD	*Exodus 16:10; Isaiah 60:1*
The Angel of the LORD	*Isaiah 37:36*
The Angel of God	*Exodus 14:19*
He is Adonai – Lord	*Isaiah 6:1*
The Holy One of God	*John 6:69*
The Holy One of Israel	*Isaiah 1:4 and 5:24*
The Holy One	*Isaiah 30:11*
The Light of the LORD	*Isaiah 2:5*
The Light of Life	*John 8:12*
The Branch	*Isaiah 4:2; Jeremiah 23:5*
King	*Isaiah 6:5, 44:6; Jeremiah 23:5*
The LORD our Righteousness	*Jeremiah 23:6*
Capstone	*Psalm 118:22*
Precious Cornerstone	*Isaiah 28:16*

Living Stone	*I Peter 2:4*
Rock	*Isaiah 8:14, 17:10*
Wonderful Counselor	*Isaiah 9:7*
Mighty God	*Isaiah 9:7*
Everlasting Father	*Isaiah 9:7*
Prince of Peace	*Isaiah 9:7*
Root of Jesse	*Isaiah 11:10*
Banner	*Isaiah 11:10, 49:22*
I Am He	*Isaiah 43:13; John 18:5*
The Arm of the LORD	*Isaiah 53:1*
Righteous Servant	*Isaiah 53:11*
Angel of His Presence	*Isaiah 63:9*
Light	*Isaiah 9:2, 42:6*
Righteous One	*Isaiah 24:16*
Light of Israel	*Isaiah 10:17*
Yeshua - Savior - Jesus	*Matthew 1:21*
Salvation	*Isaiah 52:10; Luke 2:29-32*
Savior	*Isaiah 62:11; Zechariah 9:9;*
High Priest	*Psalm 110:4; Zechariah 6:12-13; John 4:42; Titus 2:13; Hebrews 5:5-6*

www.ingramcontent.com/pod-product-compliance
Lightning Source LLC
Chambersburg PA
CBHW030323080526
44584CB00012B/681